THE STRAIGHT MIND

AND OTHER ESSAYS

THE STRAIGHT MIND

AND OTHER ESSAYS

MONIQUE WITTIG

Foreword by Louise Turcotte

Beacon Press • Boston

Beacon Press
25 Beacon Street
Boston, Massachusetts 02108-2892

Beacon Press books
are published under the auspices of
the Unitarian Universalist Association of Congregations.

99 98 97 96 95 94 93 92   8 7 6 5 4 3 2

Text design by Linda Koegel

With the exception of "The Point of View: Universal or Particular?" and
"The Site of Action," all of the essays in this volume were written in
English and were first published in the following:
"The Category of Sex," *Feminist Issues* 2, no. 2 (Spring 1982); "One Is
Not Born a Woman," *Feminist Issues* 1, no. 2 (Winter 1981); "The Straight
Mind," *Feminist Issues* 1, no. 1 (Summer 1980); "On the Social Contract,"
Feminist Issues 9, no. 1 (Spring 1989); "Homo Sum," *Feminist Issues* 10,
no. 2 (Summer 1990); "The Point of View: Universal or Particular?"
originally published as "Avant-note" to *La Passion* by Djuna Barnes (Paris:
Ed. Flammarion, 1982), translated in *Feminist Issues* 1, no. 1 (Summer
1980); "The Trojan Horse," *Feminist Issues* 4, no. 2 (Fall 1984); "The
Mark of Gender," *Feminist Issues* 5, no. 2 (Fall 1985); "The Site of
Action," trans. Lois Oppenheim in *Three Decades of the French New Novel*
(Chicago: University of Illinois Press, 1986), originally published as "Le
lieu de l'action," *Diagraphe* 32 (1984).

Library of Congress Cataloging-in-Publication Data

Wittig, Monique.
    The straight mind and other essays / Monique Wittig; foreword
by Louise Turcotte.
       p. cm.
    Includes bibliographical references.
    ISBN 0-8070-7916-2. — ISBN 0-8070-7917-0 (pbk.)
    1. Feminist theory. 2. Lesbianism. 3. Radicalism.
4. Feminism and literature.   I. Title.
HQ1190.W58   1992
305.42'01 — dc20   91-18409
                                                         CIP

Contents

Acknowledgments

I would like to thank Mary Jo Lakeland, Susan Ellis Wolf, Sande Zeig, Louise Turcotte, Pascale Noizet, Suzette Triton, Romany Eveleigh, Andrew Hrycyna, Beacon Press, and Susan Meigs for their help and support.

Foreword

CHANGING THE POINT OF VIEW

If a single name has been associated with the French Women's Liberation Movement, it is surely that of Monique Wittig. Her reputation is largely due to her literary works, which have been translated into several languages. But if Monique Wittig has made her mark as a writer in this second half of the twentieth century, the spreading of her theoretical texts will also show her to be one of the great thinkers of our time.

It is impossible to locate Wittig's influence entirely in literature, politics, or theory, for her work in fact traverses all three, and it is precisely from this multidimensionality that the great importance of her thought derives.

Much has been written about her literary works, yet not enough has been said of her theoretical and political writings. This will be a more political testimony, then, for I have been very fortunate in knowing Monique Wittig personally since the early 1970s. While it is possible to articulate the immediate influence of Wittig's thinking, it is still quite difficult to anticipate the full influence her work will have on the history of women's struggle for liberation. Her essays call into question some of the basic premises of contemporary feminist theory. What is at issue here is a total conceptual revolution.

TRANSLATED BY MARLENE WILDEMAN

In 1978, at the Modern Language Association's annual conference in New York, when Monique Wittig concluded her presentation "The Straight Mind" with the statement, "lesbians are not women," the audience's warm reception was preceded by a moment of stunned silence. When this essay was published two years later in the French journal *Questions féministes,* this stunned silence had been transformed — by some of the more radical feminists — into political pressure; a note had been added to "soften" the conclusion. Wittig's startling point of view was unimaginable at that time. In point of fact, a page had been turned in the history of the Women's Liberation Movement by one of France's principal instigators. What exactly was this page? Why was it no longer possible to see the Women's Liberation Movement in exactly the same way? Precisely because the point of view had shifted.

Since the beginning of this century, the entire women's struggle, from the defense of "women's rights" to a feminist analysis of "women's oppression," has taken as its foundation "the point of view of women." That went without saying. This analysis was refined over the years and different tendencies emerged, as happens in all liberation movements, but never was this basic consensus called into question. It seemed, in any case, indisputable. And so it was that the statement "lesbians are not women" would, at one and the same time, theoretically and politically disrupt an entire movement.

Founded upon the latest concepts of materialist and radical feminism, among them the idea of "classes of sex," Wittig's statement called into question a fundamental point feminism had never disputed: heterosexuality. Not as sexuality anymore, but as a political regime. Until then, feminism had considered the "patriarchy" an ideological system based on the domination of the class of men over the class of women. But the categories themselves, "man" and "woman," had not actually been questioned. Here is where "lesbian existence" takes on its particular meaning, for if these two categories cannot exist without each other, and lesbians exist by and for "women" only, there has to be a flaw in this conceptual system.

In the early 1980s, many lesbians in France and Quebec began calling this point of view "radical lesbianism" and totally revised their strategy. Radical lesbians have now reached a basic consensus that views heterosexuality as a political regime which must be overthrown, and we all draw inspiration from the writings of Monique Wittig. For us, Wittig's body of work constituted a point of departure for analysis and action. All of history was to be reexamined.

When history is reexamined from this point of view, it is interesting to note that the groundwork of a critique of heterosexuality as a "political institution" had already been laid at the beginning of the 1970s by certain lesbian separatists in the United States.[1] But American lesbian separatism did not take up this analysis. Rather its aim was to develop within an essentialist framework new lesbian values within lesbian communities. This was, and still is, to ignore that "heterosexuality . . . can ensure its political power only through the destruction or the negation of lesbianism."[2] The existence of lesbian communities is strategically necessary. But if they are not within the context of a political movement that aims to abolish the heterosexual system, their significance is entirely different; it is a matter then of creating a "new category." But only the destruction of the existing categories can bring about real change. This is what we have come to understand through Monique Wittig's work: it is not a question of replacing "woman" by "lesbian," but rather of making use of our strategic position to destroy the heterosexual system. "We [lesbians] . . . are runaway slaves . . . escapees from our class" ("One Is Not Born a Woman"). This key sentence provides the political dimension of the lesbian point of view. When reading Wittig, it must always be borne in mind.

In the United States, Adrienne Rich put forward a feminist analysis of heterosexuality in her 1980 essay "Compulsory Heterosexuality and Lesbian Existence."[3] For Rich, heterosexuality is "something that has to be imposed, managed, organized, propagandized and maintained by force."[4] This text poses heterosexuality as a political institution in the patriarchal system. Rich sees lesbian existence as an act of resistance to this institution, but for "lesbian existence to realize this political content in an ultimately liberating form, the erotic choice must depend and expand into conscious woman-identification."[5] Rich analyses the concept of heterosexuality within the framework of contemporary feminist theory from the "women's point of view," whereas radical lesbianism does without that point of view. It sees lesbianism as necessarily political and considers it outside the whole heterosexual political regime. For to speak of "compulsory heterosexuality" is redundant.

"Consciousness of oppression is not only a reaction to [fight against] oppression. It is also the whole conceptual reevaluation of the social world, its whole reorganization with new concepts . . ." ("One Is Not Born a Woman"). For me this summarizes the work of Monique Wittig. It was through militant groups that I came to know her. Her deep respect for each individual, her deep contempt for all forms of power, have forever altered my conception of militancy. And it is through her writing that I have also come to understand the necessity of going back and forth between the theoretical and the political. Political struggle cannot be conceived without this, and, as theory is gradually transformed, we must also transform our political struggle. This is a challenge that requires constant vigilance and a constant willingness to reconsider our actions and our political positions. It is in this sense that radical lesbians' questioning of the feminist movement must be understood.

"We must produce a political transformation of the key concepts, that is of the concepts which are strategic for us" ("The Straight Mind"). By not questioning the heterosexual political regime, contemporary feminism proposes rearranging rather than eliminating this system. Likewise, the contemporary development of the notion of "gender," it seems to me, masks, or camouflages, the relationships of oppression. Often "gender," even as it attempts to describe the social relations between men and women, lets us ignore, or diminish, the notion of "classes of sex," thereby divesting these relationships of their political dimension.

I would like to mention here one of the critical elements of Wittig's body of thought, neatly summarized by the following phrase: "A text by a minority writer is effective only if it succeeds in making the minority point of view universal" ("The Universal and the Particular"). This exemplifies Wittig's extraordinary effectiveness. In claiming the lesbian point of view as universal, she overturns the concepts to which we are accustomed. For up to this point, minority writers had to add "the universal" to their points of view if they wished to attain the unquestioned universality of the dominant class. Gay men, for example, have always defined themselves as a minority and never questioned, despite their transgression, the dominant choice. This is why gay culture has always had a fairly wide audience. Wittig's lesbian thought does not aim to transgress but clearly to do away with the categories of gender and sex on which the very notion of universality rests. "Sexes (gender), difference between the sexes, man, woman, race, black, white, nature are at the core of [the straight mind's] set of parameters. They have shaped our concepts, our laws, our institutions, our history, our cultures" ("Homo Sum"). To reexamine the parameters on which universal thought is founded requires a reevaluation of all the basic tools of analysis, including dialectics. Not in order to discard it, but to make it more effective.

Monique Wittig's work is the perfect illustration of the connection between politics and theory. Too often, we perceive these two fundamental elements as separate entities; on one side, there is the theoretical work and on the other the political, working in parallel, when in fact they should intersect. This meeting of theory and politics is fundamental for all political struggle, and it is precisely what makes Wittig's thought so disturbing. Theoretical agreement calls for political struggle. When theoretical agreement is reached, the course of history has already been shaken.

Louise Turcotte
Member of Amazones d'hier, Lesbiennes d'aujourd'hui

Materialist lesbianism, this is what I would call the political and philosophical approach of the first half of this collection of essays. I describe heterosexuality not as an institution but as a political regime which rests on the submission and the appropriation of women. In desperate straits, exactly as it was for serfs and slaves, women may "choose" to be runaways and try to escape their class or group (as lesbians do), and/or to renegotiate daily, and term by term, the social contract. There is no escape (for there is no territory, no other side of the Mississippi, no Palestine, no Liberia for women). The only thing to do is to stand on one's own feet as an escapee, a fugitive slave, a lesbian. One must accept that my point of view may appear crude, and no wonder, considering all the centuries it has had against it. First one must step out of the tracks of politics, philosophy, anthropology, history, "cultures," to understand what is really happening. Then one might have to do without the munificent philosophical toy of dialectics, because it does not allow one to conceive of the opposition of men and women in terms of class conflict. One must understand that this conflict has nothing eternal about it and that to overcome it one must destroy politically, philosophically, and symbolically the categories of "men" and "women."

Dialectics has let us down. Therefore the comprehension of what "materialism" and materiality are belongs to us. Here I will list a few names, names of those without whom I would not have been empowered to attack conceptually the straight world. By order of publication of their work, Nicole-Claude Mathieu, Christine Delphy, Colette Guillaumin, Paola Tabet, Sande Zeig represent for me the most important political influences during the time I wrote these essays. Each one of them deserves a chapter.

Mathieu was the first to establish women in the social sciences as a sociological and anthropological entity, that is, not as appendages to men, but as a group which stands on its own. She is the originator of what she has called the anthropology of the sexes. But she is a philosopher as well as an anthropologist in the French tradition. Her last essay on consciousness is a landmark. Mathieu gives us the missing link in the history of consciousness by providing an analysis of consciousness as oppressed — which does not mean consciousness as alienated.

Delphy coined the expression "materialist feminism," and she changed the Marxist concept of class, showing it to be obsolete since it does not take into account the kind of work that has no exchange value, work that represents two thirds of the work provided globally, according to recent figures of the United Nations.

Guillaumin transformed the point of view on materialism and materiality in such a way that after her it cannot be recognized. One has to read Guillaumin to understand that what we have called materialism until now was very far from the mark, since the most important aspect of materiality was ignored. There is, *material*:

on the one hand, the physical and mental exertion attached to the kind of work that is merely physical service to one or several persons without any compensation in wages, and, on the other hand, the physical and mental implications of the kind of work that robs the whole person of herself night and day. But Guillaumin is more widely known to have defined the double aspect of the oppression of women: a private appropriation by an individual (a husband or a father) and a collective appropriation of the whole group, including celibate individuals by the class of men. In other words, "sexage." If you are unmarried, you will have to be available to take care of the sick, the aged, the weak, (as nuns and volunteer workers do), whether they belong to your family or not.

Tabet, in working in the anthropology of the sexes, has provided a link between women as collectively appropriated. Particularly in her last works on prostitution, she shows that there is a continuum between so-called prostitutes and lesbians as a class of women who are not privately appropriated but are still collectively the object of heterosexual oppression.

Zeig, with whom I wrote *Lesbian Peoples: Material for a Dictionary* and the play *The Constant Journey,* made me understand that the effects of oppression on the body — giving it its form, its gestures, its movement, its motricity, and even its muscles — have their origin in the abstract domain of concepts, through the words that formalize them. I was thinking of her work as an actor and as a writer when I said (in "The Mark of Gender") that "language casts sheaves of reality upon the social body, stamping it and violently shaping it, for example, the bodies of social actors . . ."

There are many other important names I have not mentioned

materiality of opression— inscription on body

(Colette Capitan, Monique Plaza, Emmanuelle de Lesseps, Louise Turcotte, Danièle Charest, Suzette Triton, Claudie Lesselier, etc). But I am only enumerating the people who had a direct influence on my way of thinking.

These collected essays are divided in two parts. The first half, as I have already mentioned, is a political discussion. With "Category of Sex" I wanted to show "sex" as a political category. The word "gender" already used in England and in the United States seemed to me imprecise. In "One Is Not Born a Woman," there is an attempt to establish a link between women fighting for women as a class, against the idea of "woman" as an essentialist concept. In the "Straight Mind," I sketch the thought which throughout the centuries built heterosexuality as a given. "The Social Contract" discusses the idea that there is an issue beyond the heterosexual social contract. "Homo Sum" is about political thought and the future of dialectics.

In the second half of this collection I mention the object of my main concern: writing. My first book, *The Opoponax,* was supported by the French New Novel, a school of writers whom I will always admire for the way they have revolutionized the novel and for their stand for literature as literature. They have taught me what work is in literature.

In "The Point of View, Universal or Particular" I touch upon the problem of a work of art in which the literary forms cannot be perceived because the theme of the work (here homosexuality) predominates.

The "Trojan Horse" is a discussion of language as raw material for the writer and of how violently literary forms affect their context when they are new. This essay has been developed in an unpublished work which I call *The Literary Workshop (le Chantier littéraire).*

In "Mark of Gender" I examine the original meaning of gender and how it represents the linguistic index of women's material oppression.

"The Site of Action" focuses on language as the ultimate social contract, an idea that Nathalie Sarraute's work inspired.

Different journals have been involved in publishing texts on the new materialism. The first was *Questions féministes,* whose collective invited me to join them when I first came to the United States. At that time I worked on the preparation of a series of seminars in the French Department at the University of California, Berkeley. I was trying to inaugurate on my own an epistemological revolution in the approach to the oppression of women. It was then that I joined with enthusiasm this group whose members were working in the same direction.

Feminist Issues was begun in Berkeley a few years later to address the concept of feminist materialism, and their collective invited me to be their advisory editor. In spite of the conflict we had in France on the lesbian question, the American editors (Mary Jo Lakeland and Susan Ellis Wolf) decided that this question would not injure the journal and that it would receive the attention that it deserved in an international framework.

Amazones d'hier, Lesbiennes d'aujourd'hui was published in Montreal by radical lesbians led by Louise Turcotte and Danièle Charest who understood both the necessity of a theory of feminist materialism and the necessity of going beyond it, through the theory and the struggle that they have adopted and developed.

Monique Wittig
Tucson
January 1991

for tuesday

THE CATEGORY OF SEX

1976 / 1982

*O. expresses a virile idea. Virile or at least masculine. At last a
woman who admits it! Who admits what? Something that women
have always till now refused to admit (and today more than ever
before). Something that men have always reproached them with: that
they never cease obeying their nature, the call of their blood, that
everything in them, even their minds, is sex.*
— Jean Paulhan, "Happiness in Slavery,"
preface to *The Story of O*, by Pauline de Réage

*In the course of the year 1838, the peaceful island of Barbados was
rocked by a strange and bloody revolt. About two hundred Negroes
of both sexes, all of whom had recently been emancipated by the
Proclamation of March, came one morning to beg their former
master, a certain Glenelg, to take them back into bondage. . . . I
suspect . . . that Glenelg's slaves were in love with their master, that
they couldn't bear to be without him.*
— Jean Paulhan, "Happiness in Slavery"

*What should I be getting married for? I find life good enough as it is.
What do I need a wife for? . . . And what's so good about a woman?
— A woman is a worker. A woman is a man's servant. — But what
would I be needing a worker for? — That's just it. You like to have
others pulling your chestnuts out of the fire. . . . — Well, marry me
off, if that's the case.*
— Ivan Turgenev, *The Hunting Sketches*

The perenniality of the sexes and the perenniality of slaves and masters proceed from the same belief, and, as there are no slaves without masters, there are no women without men. The ideology of sexual difference functions as censorship in our culture by masking, on the ground of nature, the social opposition between men and women. Masculine/feminine, male/female are the categories which serve to conceal the fact that social differences always belong to an economic, political, ideological order. Every system of domination establishes divisions at the material and economic level. Furthermore, the divisions are abstracted and turned into concepts by the masters, and later on by the slaves when they rebel and start to struggle. The masters explain and justify the established divisions as a result of natural differences. The slaves, when they rebel and start to struggle, read social oppositions into the so-called natural differences.

For there is no sex. There is but sex that is oppressed and sex that oppresses. It is oppression that creates sex and not the contrary. The contrary would be to say that sex creates oppression, or to say that the cause (origin) of oppression is to be found in sex itself, in a natural division of the sexes preexisting (or outside of) society.

The primacy of difference so constitutes our thought that it prevents turning inward on itself to question itself, no matter how necessary that may be to apprehend the basis of that which precisely constitutes it. To apprehend a difference in dialectical terms is to make apparent the contradictory terms to be resolved. To understand social reality in dialectical materialist terms is to apprehend the oppositions between classes, term to term, and make them meet under the same copula (a conflict in the social order), which is also a resolution (an abolition in the social order) of the apparent contradictions.

The class struggle is precisely that which resolves the contradictions between two opposed classes by abolishing them at the same time that it constitutes and reveals them as classes. The class struggle between women and men, which should be undertaken by all women, is that which resolves the contradictions between the sexes, abolishing them at the same time that it makes them understood. We must notice that the contradictions always belong to a material order. The important idea for me is that before the conflict (rebellion, struggle) there are no categories of opposition but only of difference. And it is not until the struggle breaks out that the violent reality of the oppositions and the political nature of the differences become manifest. For as long as oppositions (differences) appear as given, already there, before all thought, "natural" — as long as there is no conflict and no struggle — there is no dialectic, there is no change, no movement. The dominant thought refuses to turn inward on itself to apprehend that which questions it.

And, indeed, as long as there is no women's struggle, there is no conflict between men and women. It is the fate of women to perform three-quarters of the work of society (in the public as well as in the private domain) plus the bodily work of reproduction according to a preestablished rate. Being murdered, mutilated, physically and mentally tortured and abused, being raped, being battered, and being forced to marry is the fate of women. And fate supposedly cannot be changed. Women do not know that they are totally dominated by men, and when they acknowledge the fact, they can "hardly believe it." And often, as a last recourse before the bare and crude reality, they refuse to "believe" that men dominate them with full knowledge (for oppression is far more hideous for the oppressed than for the oppressors). Men, on the other hand, know perfectly well that they are dominating women ("We are the masters of women," said André Breton[1]) and are trained to do it. They do not need to express it all the time, for one can scarcely talk of domination over what one owns.

What is this thought which refuses to reverse itself, which never puts into question what primarily constitutes it? This thought is the dominant thought. It is a thought which affirms an "already there" of the sexes, something which is supposed to have come before all thought, before all society. This thought is the thought of those who rule over women.

The ideas of the ruling class are in every epoch the ruling ideas, i.e. the class which is the ruling *material* force of society, is at the same time its ruling *intellectual* force. The class which has the means of material production at its disposal, has control at the same time over the means of mental production, so that thereby, generally speaking, the ideas of those who lack the means of mental production are subject to it. The ruling ideas are nothing more than the ideal expression of the dominant material relationships, the dominant material relationships grasped as ideas: hence of the relationships which make the one class the ruling one, therefore, the ideas of its dominance. (Marx and Engels, *The German Ideology*)

This thought based on the primacy of difference is the thought of domination.

Dominance provides women with a body of data, of givens, of a prioris, which, all the more for being questionable, form a huge political construct, a tight network that affects everything, our thoughts, our gestures, our acts, our work, our feelings, our relationships.

Dominance thus teaches us from all directions:

—that there are before all thinking, all society, "sexes" (two categories of individuals born) with a constitutive difference, a difference that has ontological consequences (the metaphysical approach),

—that there are before all thinking, all social order, "sexes" with a "natural" or "biological" or "hormonal" or "genetic" difference that has sociological consequences (the scientific approach),

—that there is before all thinking, all social order, a "natural division of labor in the family," a "division of labor [that] was originally nothing *but* the division of labor in the sexual act" (the Marxist approach).

Whatever the approach, the idea remains basically the same. The sexes, in spite of their constitutive difference, must inevitably develop relationships from category to category. Belonging to the natural order, these relationships cannot be spoken of as social relationships. This thought which impregnates all discourses, including common-sense ones (Adam's rib or Adam *is,* Eve is Adam's rib), is the thought of domination. Its body of discourses is constantly reinforced on all levels of social reality and conceals the political fact of the subjugation of one sex by the other, the compulsory character of the category itself (which constitutes the first definition of the social being in civil status). The category of sex does not exist a priori, before all society. And as a category of dominance it cannot be a product of natural dominance but of the social dominance of women by men, for there is but social dominance.

The category of sex is the political category that founds society as heterosexual. As such it does not concern being but relationships (for women and men are the result of relationships), although the two aspects are always confused when they are discussed. The category of sex is the one that rules as "natural" the relation that is at the base of (heterosexual) society and through which half of the population, women, are "heterosexualized" (the making of women is like the making of eunuchs, the breeding of slaves, of animals) and submitted to a heterosexual economy. For the category of sex is the product of a heterosexual society which imposes on women the rigid obligation of the reproduction of the "species," that is, the reproduction of heterosexual society. The compulsory reproduction of the "species" by women is the system of exploitation on which heterosexuality is economically based. Reproduction is essentially that work, that production by women, through which the appropriation by men of all the work of women proceeds. One must include here the appropriation of work which is associated "by nature" with reproduction, the raising of children and domestic chores. This appropriation of the work of women is effected in the same way as the appropriation of the work of the working class by the ruling class. It cannot be said that one of these two productions (reproduction) is "natural" while the other one is social. This argument is only the theoretical, ideological justification of oppression, an argument to make women believe that before society and in all societies they are subject to this obligation to reproduce. However, as we know nothing about work, about social production, outside of the context of exploitation, we know nothing about the reproduction of society outside of its context of exploitation.

The category of sex is the product of a heterosexual society in which men appropriate for themselves the reproduction and production of women and also their physical persons by means of a contract called the marriage contract. Compare this contract with the contract that binds a worker to his employer. The contract binding the woman to the man is in principle a contract for life, which only law can break (divorce). It assigns the woman certain obligations, including unpaid work. The work (housework, raising children) and the obligations (surrender of her reproduction in the name of her husband, cohabitation by day and night, forced coitus, assignment of residence implied by the legal concept of "surrender of the conjugal domicile") mean in their terms a surrender by the woman of her physical person to her husband. That the woman depends directly on her husband is implicit in the police's policy of not intervening when a husband beats his wife. The police intervene with the specific charge of assault and battery when one citizen beats another citizen. But a woman who has signed a marriage contract has thereby ceased to be an ordinary citizen (protected by law). The police openly express their aversion to getting involved in domestic affairs (as opposed to civil affairs), where the authority of the state does not have to intervene directly since it is relayed through that of the husband. One has to go to shelters for battered women to see how far this authority can be exercised.

The category of sex is the product of heterosexual society that turns half of the population into sexual beings, for sex is a category which women cannot be outside of. Wherever they are, whatever they do (including working in the public sector), they are seen (and made) sexually available to men, and they, breasts, buttocks, costume, must be visible. They must wear their yellow star, their constant smile, day and night. One might consider that every woman, married or not, has a period of forced sexual service, a sexual service which we may compare to the military one, and which can vary between a day, a year, or twenty-five years or more. Some lesbians and nuns escape, but they are very few, although the number is growing. Although women are very visible as sexual beings, as social beings they are totally invisible, and as such must appear as little as possible, and always with some kind of excuse if they do so. One only has to read interviews with outstanding women to hear them apologizing. And the newspapers still today report that "two students and a woman," "two lawyers and a woman," "three travelers and a woman" were seen doing this or that. For the category of sex is the category that sticks to women, for only they cannot be conceived of outside of it. Only *they* are sex, *the* sex, and sex they have been made in their minds, bodies, acts, gestures; even their murders and beatings are sexual. Indeed, the category of sex tightly holds women.

For the category of sex is a totalitarian one, which to prove true has its inquisitions, its courts, its tribunals, its body of laws, its terrors, its tortures, its mutilations, its executions, its police. It shapes the mind as well as the body since it controls all mental production. It grips our minds in such a way that we cannot think outside of it. This is why we must destroy it and start thinking beyond it if we want to start thinking at all, as we must destroy the sexes as a sociological reality if we want to start to exist. The category of sex is the category that ordains slavery for women, and it works specifically, as it did for black slaves, through an operation of reduction, by taking the part for the whole, a part (color, sex) through which the whole human group has to pass as through a screen. Notice that in civil matters color as well as sex still must be "declared." However, because of the abolition of slavery, the "declaration" of "color" is now considered discriminatory. But that does not hold true for the "declaration" of "sex," which not even women dream of abolishing. I say: it is about time to do so.[2]

ONE IS NOT BORN A WOMAN

1981

A materialist feminist[1] approach to women's oppression destroys
the idea that women are a "natural group": "a racial group of
a special kind, a group perceived *as natural,* a group of men
considered as materially specific in their bodies."[2] What the analysis accomplishes on the level of ideas, practice makes actual at
the level of facts: by its very existence, lesbian society destroys
the artificial (social) fact constituting women as a "natural
group." A lesbian society[3] pragmatically reveals that the division
from men of which women have been the object is a political
one and shows that we have been ideologically rebuilt into a
"natural group." In the case of women, ideology goes far since
our bodies as well as our minds are the product of this manipulation. We have been compelled in our bodies and in our minds
to correspond, feature by feature, with the *idea* of nature that
has been established for us. Distorted to such an extent that our
deformed body is what they call "natural," what is supposed to
exist as such before oppression. Distorted to such an extent that
in the end oppression seems to be a consequence of this "nature"
within ourselves (a nature which is only an *idea*). What a materialist analysis does by reasoning, a lesbian society accomplishes practically: not only is there no natural group "women"

(we lesbians are living proof of it), but as individuals as well we question "woman," which for us, as for Simone de Beauvoir, is only a myth. She said: "One is not born, but becomes a woman. No biological, psychological, or economic fate determines the figure that the human female presents in society: it is civilization as a whole that produces this creature, intermediate between male and eunuch, which is described as feminine."[4]

However, most of the feminists and lesbian-feminists in America and elsewhere still believe that the basis of women's oppression *is biological as well as* historical. Some of them even claim rces in Simone de Beauvoir.[5] The belief in mother prehistory" when women created civilization (be-gical predisposition) while the coarse and brutal cause of a biological predisposition) is symmet-iologizing interpretation of history produced up lass of men. It is still the same method of finding men a biological explanation of their division, l facts. For me this could never constitute a les-to women's oppression, since it assumes that the basis of society or the beginning of society lies in heterosexuality. Matriarchy is no less heterosexual than patriarchy: it is only the sex of the oppressor that changes. Furthermore, not only is this conception still imprisoned in the categories of sex (woman and man), but it holds onto the idea that the capacity to give birth (biology) is what defines a woman. Although practical facts and ways of living contradict this theory in lesbian society, there are lesbians who affirm that "women and men are different species or races (the words are used interchangeably): men are biologically inferior to women; male violence is a biological inevitability . . ."[6] By doing this, by admitting that there is a "natural"

division between women and men, we naturalize history, we assume that "men" and "women" have always existed and will
always exist. Not only do we naturalize history, but also con-
sequently we naturalize the social phenomena which express our
oppression, making change impossible. For example, instead of
seeing giving birth as a forced production, we see it as a "natural," "biological" process, forgetting that in our societies births
are planned (demography), forgetting that we ourselves are programmed to produce children, while this is the only social activity "short of war"[7] that presents such a great danger of death.
Thus, as long as we will be "unable to abandon by will or im-
pulse a lifelong and centuries-old commitment to childbearing
as *the* female creative act,"[8] gaining control of the production of
children will mean much more than the mere control of the material means of this production: women will have to abstract
themselves from the definition "woman" which is imposed upon
them.

A materialist feminist approach shows that what we take for the
cause or origin of oppression is in fact only the *mark*[9] imposed
by the oppressor: the "myth of woman,"[10] plus its material effects and manifestations in the(appropriated)consciousness and
bodies of women. Thus, this mark does not predate oppression:
Colette Guillaumin has shown that before the socioeconomic
reality of black slavery, the concept of race did not exist, at least
not in its modern meaning, since it was applied to the lineage of
families. However, now, race, exactly like sex, is taken as an
"immediate given," a "sensible given," "physical features," belonging to a natural order. But what we believe to be a physical
and direct perception is only a sophisticated and mythic con-

struction, an "imaginary formation,"[11] which reinterprets physical features (in themselves as neutral as any others but marked by the social system) through the network of relationships in which they are perceived. (They are seen as *black*, therefore they *are* black; they are seen as *women*, therefore, they *are* women. But before being *seen* that way, they first had to be *made* that way.) Lesbians should always remember and acknowledge how "unnatural," compelling, totally oppressive, and destructive being "woman" was for us in the old days before the women's liberation movement. It was a political constraint, and those who resisted it were accused of not being "real" women. But then we were proud of it, since in the accusation there was already something like a shadow of victory: the avowal by the oppressor that "woman" is not something that goes without saying, since to be one, one has to be a "real" one. We were at the same time accused of wanting to be men. Today this double accusation has been taken up again with enthusiasm in the context of the women's liberation movement by some feminists and also, alas, by some lesbians whose political goal seems somehow to be becoming more and more "feminine." To refuse to be a woman, however, does not mean that one has to become a man. Besides, if we take as an example the perfect "butch," the classic example which provokes the most horror, whom Proust would have called a woman/man, how is her alienation different from that of someone who wants to become a woman? Tweedledum and Tweedledee. At least for a woman, wanting to become a man proves that she has escaped her initial programming. But even if she would like to, with all her strength, she cannot become a man. For becoming a man would demand from a woman not only a man's external appearance but his consciousness as

Lesbians exist as a "third gender" thru stabilization of "woman" and "man"? How does sex not exist if lesbian identity is a refusal of male dominance?

well, that is, the consciousness of one who disp[...] at least two "natural" slaves during his life spar[...] sible, and one feature of lesbian oppression con[...] making women out of reach for us, since women[...] Thus a lesbian *has to* be something else, a not[...] man, a product of society, not a product of nat[...] no nature in society.

The refusal to become (or to remain) heterosexual always meant to refuse to become a man or a woman, consciously or not. For a lesbian this goes further than the refusal of the *role* "woman." It is the refusal of the economic, ideological, and political power of a man. This, we lesbians, and nonlesbians as well, knew before the beginning of the lesbian and feminist movement. However, as Andrea Dworkin emphasizes, many lesbians recently "have increasingly tried to transform the very ideology that has enslaved us into a dynamic, religious, psychologically compelling celebration of female biological potential."[12] Thus, some avenues of the feminist and lesbian movement lead us back to the myth of woman which was created by men especially for us, and with it we sink back into a natural group. Having stood up to fight for a sexless society,[13] we now find ourselves entrapped in the familiar deadlock of "woman is wonderful." Simone de Beauvoir underlined particularly the false consciousness which consists of selecting among the features of the myth (that women are different from men) those which look good and using them as a definition for women. What the concept "woman is wonderful" accomplishes is that it retains for defining women the best features (best according to whom?) which oppression has granted us, and it does not radically question the categories "man" and "woman," which are political categories and not natural givens. It puts us in a position of fighting within the class "women" not as the other classes do, for the disappearance of our class, but for the defense of "woman" and its reenforcement. It leads us to develop with complacency "new" theories about our specificity: thus, we call our passivity "nonviolence," when the main and emergent point for us is to fight our passivity (our fear, rather, a justified one). The ambiguity of the term "feminist" sums up the whole situation. What does "feminist" mean? Feminist is formed with the word "femme," "woman," and means: someone who fights for women. For many of us it means someone who fights for women as a class and for the disappearance of this class. For many others it means someone who fights for woman and her defense — for the myth, then, and its reenforcement. But why was the word "feminist" chosen if it retains the least ambiguity? We chose to call ourselves "feminists" ten years ago, not in order to support or reenforce the myth of woman, nor to identify ourselves with the oppressor's definition of us, but rather to affirm that our movement had a history and to emphasize the political link with the old feminist movement.

It is, then, this movement that we can put in question for the meaning that it gave to feminism. It so happens that feminism in the last century could never resolve its contradictions on the subject of nature/culture, woman/society. Women started to fight for themselves as a group and rightly considered that they shared common features as a result of oppression. But for them these features were natural and biological rather than social. They went so far as to adopt the Darwinist theory of evolution. They did not believe like Darwin, however, "that women were less evolved than men, but they did believe that male and female natures had diverged in the course of evolutionary development and that society at large reflected this polarization."[14] "The failure of early feminism was that it only attacked the Darwinist charge of female inferiority, while accepting the foundations of this charge — namely, the view of woman as 'unique.'"[15] And finally it was women scholars — and not feminists — who scientifically destroyed this theory. But the early feminists had failed to regard history as a dynamic process which develops from conflicts of interests. Furthermore, they still believed as men do that the cause (origin) of their oppression lay within themselves. And therefore after some astonishing victories the feminists of this first front found themselves at an impasse out of a lack of reasons to fight. They upheld the illogical principle of "equality in difference," an idea now being born again. They fell back into the trap which threatens us once again: the myth of woman.

marxism

Thus it is our historical task, and only ours, to define what we call oppression in materialist terms, to make it evident that women are a class, which is to say that the category "woman" as well as the category "man" are political and economic categories not eternal ones. Our fight aims to suppress men as a class, not through a genocidal, but a political struggle. Once the class "men" disappears, "women" as a class will disappear as well, for there are no slaves without masters. Our first task, it seems, is to always thoroughly dissociate "women" (the class within which we fight) and "woman," the myth. For "woman" does not exist for us: it is only an imaginary formation, while "women" is the product of a social relationship. We felt this strongly when everywhere we refused to be called a "*woman's* liberation movement." Furthermore, we have to destroy the myth inside and outside ourselves. "Woman" is not each one of us, but the political

"woman" designates the myth
"women" the class

and ideological formation which negates "women" (the product of a relation of exploitation). "Woman" is there to confuse us, to hide the reality "women." In order to be aware of being a class and to become a class we first have to kill the myth of "woman" including its most seductive aspects (I think about Virginia Woolf when she said the first task of a woman writer is to kill "the angel in the house"). But to become a class we do not have to suppress our individual selves, and since no individual can be reduced to her/his oppression we are also confronted with the historical necessity of constituting ourselves as the individual subjects of our history as well. I believe this is the reason why all these attempts at "new" definitions of woman are blossoming now. What is at stake (and of course not only for women) is an individual definition as well as a class definition. For once one has acknowledged oppression, one needs to know and experience the fact that one can constitute oneself as a subject (as opposed to an object of oppression), that one can become *someone* in spite of oppression, that one has one's own identity. There is no possible fight for someone deprived of an identity, no internal motivation for fighting, since, although I can fight only with others, first I fight for myself. *Anti-Butler*

humanist

The question of the individual subject is historically a difficult one for everybody. Marxism, the last avatar of materialism, the science which has politically formed us, does not want to hear anything about a "subject." Marxism has rejected the transcendental subject, the subject as constitutive of knowledge, the "pure" consciousness. All that thinks per se, before all experience, has ended up in the garbage can of history, because it claimed to exist outside matter, prior to matter, and needed God, spirit, or soul to exist in such a way. This is what is called "idealism." As for individuals, they are only the product of social relations, therefore their consciousness can only be "alienated." (Marx, in *The German Ideology,* says precisely that individuals of the dominating class are also alienated, although they are the direct producers of the ideas that alienate the classes oppressed by them. But since they draw visible advantages from their own alienation they can bear it without too much suffering.) There exists such a thing as class consciousness, but a consciousness which does not refer to a particular subject, except as participating in general conditions of exploitation at the same time as the other subjects of their class, all sharing the same consciousness. As for the practical class problems — outside of the class problems as traditionally defined — that one could encounter (for example, sexual problems), they were considered "bourgeois" problems that would disappear with the final victory of the class struggle. "Individualistic," "subjectivist," "petit bourgeois," these were the labels given to any person who had shown problems which could not be reduced to the "class struggle" itself.

Thus Marxism has denied the members of oppressed classes the attribute of being a subject. In doing this, Marxism, because of the ideological and political power this "revolutionary science" immediately exercised upon the workers' movement and all other political groups, has prevented all categories of oppressed peoples from constituting themselves historically as subjects (subjects of their struggle, for example). This means that the "masses" did not fight for themselves but for *the* party or its organizations. And when an economic transformation took place (end of private property, constitution of the socialist state), no revolutionary change took place within the new society, because the people themselves did not change.

For women, Marxism had two results. It prevented them from

being aware that they are a class and therefore from constituting themselves as a class for a very long time, by leaving the relation "women/men" outside of the social order, by turning it into a natural relation, doubtless for Marxists the only one, along with the relation of mothers to children, to be seen this way, and by hiding the class conflict between men and women behind a natural division of labor (*The German Ideology*). This concerns the theoretical (ideological) level. On the practical level, Lenin, *the* party, all the communist parties up to now, including all the most radical political groups, have always reacted to any attempt on the part of women to reflect and form groups based on their own class problem with an accusation of divisiveness. By uniting, we women are dividing the strength of the people. This means that for the Marxists women *belong* either to the bourgeois class or to the proletariat class, in other words, to the men of these classes. In addition, Marxist theory does not allow women any more than other classes of oppressed people to constitute themselves as historical subjects, because Marxism does not take into account the fact that a class also consists of individuals one by one. Class consciousness is not enough. We must try to understand philosophically (politically) these concepts of "subject" and "class consciousness" and how they work in relation to our history. When we discover that women are the objects of oppression and appropriation, at the very moment that we become able to perceive this, we become subjects in the sense of cognitive subjects, through an operation of abstraction. Consciousness of oppression is not only a reaction to (fight against) oppression. It is also the whole conceptual reevaluation of the social world, its whole reorganization with new concepts, from the point of view of oppression. It is what I would call the science of oppression

[margin note: sounds like standpoint— development of consciousness]

created by the oppressed. This operation of understanding reality has to be undertaken by every one of us: call it a subjective, cognitive practice. The movement back and forth between the levels of reality (the conceptual reality and the material reality of oppression, which are both social realities) is accomplished through language.

It is we who historically must undertake the task of defining the individual subject in materialist terms. This certainly seems to be an impossibility since materialism and subjectivity have always been mutually exclusive. Nevertheless, and rather than despairing of ever understanding, we must recognize the *need* to reach subjectivity in the abandonment by many of us to the myth "woman" (the myth of woman being only a snare that holds us up). This real necessity for everyone to exist as an individual, as well as a member of a class, is perhaps the first condition for the accomplishment of a revolution, without which there can be no real fight or transformation. But the opposite is also true; without class and class consciousness there are no real subjects, only alienated individuals. For women to answer the question of the individual subject in materialist terms is first to show, as the lesbians and feminists did, that supposedly "subjective," "individual," "private" problems are in fact social problems, class problems; that sexuality is not for women an individual and subjective expression, but a social institution of violence. But once we have shown that all so-called personal problems are in fact class problems, we will still be left with the question of the subject of each singular woman — not the myth, but each one of us. At this point, let us say that a new personal and subjective definition for all humankind can only be found beyond the categories of sex (woman and man) and that the advent of individual subjects demands first destroying the categories of sex, ending the use of them, and rejecting all sciences which still use these categories as their fundamentals (practically all social sciences).

To destroy "woman" does not mean that we aim, short of physical destruction, to destroy lesbianism simultaneously with the categories of sex, because lesbianism provides for the moment the only social form in which we can live freely. Lesbian is the only concept I know of which is beyond the categories of sex (woman and man), because the designated subject (lesbian) is *not* a woman, either economically, or politically, or ideologically. For what makes a woman is a specific social relation to a man, a relation that we have previously called servitude,[16] a relation which implies personal and physical obligation as well as economic obligation ("forced residence,"[17] domestic corvée, conjugal duties, unlimited production of children, etc.), a relation which lesbians escape by refusing to become or to stay heterosexual. We are escapees from our class in the same way as the American runaway slaves were when escaping slavery and becoming free. For us this is an absolute necessity; our survival demands that we contribute all our strength to the destruction of the class of women within which men appropriate women. This can be accomplished only by the destruction of heterosexuality as a social system which is based on the oppression of women by men and which produces the doctrine of the difference between the sexes to justify this oppression.

THE STRAIGHT MIND[1]

1980

In recent years in Paris, language as a phenomenon has dominated modern theoretical systems and the social sciences and has entered the political discussions of the lesbian and women's liberation movements. This is because it relates to an important political field where what is at play is power, or more than that, a network of powers, since there is a multiplicity of languages that constantly act upon the social reality. The importance of language as such as a political stake has only recently been perceived.[2] But the gigantic development of linguistics, the multiplication of schools of linguistics, the advent of the sciences of communication, and the technicality of the metalanguages that these sciences utilize, represent the symptoms of the importance of what is politically at stake. The science of language has invaded other sciences, such as anthropology through Lévi-Strauss, psychoanalysis through Lacan, and all the disciplines which have developed from the basis of structuralism.

The early semiology of Roland Barthes nearly escaped from linguistic domination to become a political analysis of the different systems of signs, to establish a relationship between this or that system of signs — for example, the myths of the petit bourgeois class — and the class struggle within capitalism that this system tends to conceal. We were almost saved, for political semiology is a weapon (a method) that we need to analyze what is called ideology. But the miracle did not last. Rather than introducing into semiology concepts which are foreign to it — in this case Marxist concepts — Barthes quickly stated that semiology was only a branch of linguistics and that language was its only object.

Thus, the entire world is only a great register where the most diverse languages come to have themselves recorded, such as the language of the Unconscious,[3] the language of fashion, the language of the exchange of women where human beings are literally the signs which are used to communicate. These languages, or rather these discourses, fit into one another, interpenetrate one another, support one another, reinforce one another, auto-engender, and engender one another. Linguistics engenders semiology and structural linguistics, structural linguistics engenders structuralism, which engenders the Structural Unconscious. The ensemble of these discourses produces a confusing static for the oppressed, which makes them lose sight of the material cause of their oppression and plunges them into a kind of ahistoric vacuum.

For they produce a scientific reading of the social reality in which human beings are given as invariants, untouched by history and unworked by class conflicts, with identical psyches because genetically programmed. This psyche, equally untouched by history and unworked by class conflicts, provides the specialists, from the beginning of the twentieth century, with a whole arsenal of invariants: the symbolic language which very advantageously functions with very few elements, since, like digits (0-9), the symbols "unconsciously" produced by the psyche are not very numerous. Therefore, these symbols are very easy to impose, through therapy and theorization, upon the collective and individual unconscious. We are taught that the Unconscious, with perfectly good taste, structures itself upon metaphors, for example, the name-of-the-father, the Oedipus complex, castration, the murder-or-death-of-the-father, the exchange of women, etc. If the Unconscious, however, is easy to control, it is not just by anybody. Similar to mystical revelations, the apparition of symbols in the psyche demands multiple interpretations. Only specialists can accomplish the deciphering of the Unconscious. Only they, the psychoanalysts, are allowed (authorized?) to organize and interpret psychic manifestations which will show the symbol in its full meaning. And while the symbolic language is extremely poor and essentially lacunary, the languages or metalanguages which interpret it are developing, each one of them, with a richness, a display, that only theological exegeses of the Bible have equalled.

Who gave the psychoanalysts their knowledge? For example, for Lacan, what he calls the "psychoanalytic discourse," or the "analytical experience," both "teach" him what he already knows. And each one teaches him what the other one taught him. But can we deny that Lacan scientifically discovered, through the "analytical experience" (somehow an experiment), the structures of the Unconscious? Will we be irresponsible enough to disregard the discourses of the psychoanalyzed people lying on their couches? In my opinion, there is no doubt that Lacan found in the Unconscious the structures he said he found there, since he had previously put them there. People who did not fall into the power of the psychoanalytical institution may experience an immeasurable feeling of sadness at the degree of oppression (of manipulation) that the psychoanalyzed discourses show. In the analytical experience there is an oppressed person, the psychoanalyzed, whose need for communication is exploited and who (in the same way as the witches could, under torture, only repeat the language that the inquisitors wanted to hear) has no other choice, (if s/he does not want to destroy the implicit contract which allows her/him to communicate and which s/he needs), than to attempt to say what s/he is supposed to say. They say that this can last for a lifetime — cruel contract which constrains a human being to display her/his misery to an oppressor who is directly responsible for it, who exploits her/him economically, politically, ideologically and whose interpretation reduces this misery to a few figures of speech.

But can the need to communicate that this contract implies only be satisfied in the psychoanalytical situation, in being cured or "experimented" with? If we believe recent testimonies[4] by lesbians, feminists, and gay men, this is not the case. All their testimonies emphasize the political significance of the impossibility that lesbians, feminists, and gay men face in the attempt to communicate in heterosexual society, other than with a psychoanalyst. When the general state of things is understood (one is not sick or to be cured, one has an enemy) the result is that the oppressed person breaks the psychoanalytical contract. This is what appears in the testimonies, along with the teaching that the psychoanalytical contract was not a contract of consent but a forced one.

The discourses which particularly oppress all of us, lesbians, women, and homosexual men, are those which take for granted that what founds society, any society, is heterosexuality.[5] These discourses speak about us and claim to say the truth in an apolitical field, as if anything of that which signifies could escape the political in this moment of history, and as if, in what concerns us, politically insignificant signs could exist. These discourses of heterosexuality oppress us in the sense that they prevent us from speaking unless we speak in their terms. Everything which puts them into question is at once disregarded as elementary. Our refusal of the totalizing interpretation of psychoanalysis makes the theoreticians say that we neglect the symbolic dimension. These discourses deny us every possibility of creating our own categories. But their most ferocious action is the unrelenting tyranny that they exert upon our physical and mental selves.

When we use the overgeneralizing term "ideology" to designate all the discourses of the dominating group, we relegate these discourses to the domain of Irreal Ideas; we forget the material (physical) violence that they directly do to the oppressed people, a violence produced by the abstract and "scientific" discourses as well as by the discourses of the mass media. I would like to insist on the material oppression of individuals by discourses, and I would like to underline its immediate effects through the example of pornography.

Pornographic images, films, magazine photos, publicity posters on the walls of the cities, constitute a discourse, and this discourse covers our world with its signs, and this discourse has a meaning: it signifies that women are dominated. Semioticians can interpret the system of this discourse, describe its disposition. What they read in that discourse are signs whose function is not to signify and which have no *raison d'être* except to be elements of a certain system or disposition. But for us this discourse is not divorced from the real as it is for semioticians. Not only does it maintain very close relations with the social reality which is our oppression (economically and politically), but also it is in itself real since it is one of the aspects of oppression, since it exerts a precise power over us. The pornographic discourse is one of the strategies of violence which are exercised upon us: it humiliates, it degrades, it is a crime against our "humanity." As a harassing tactic it has another function, that of a warning. It orders us to stay in line, and it keeps those who would tend to forget who they are in step; it calls upon fear. These same experts in semiotics, referred to earlier, reproach us for confusing, when we demonstrate against pornography, the discourses with the reality. They do not see that this discourse *is* reality for us, one of the facets of the reality of our oppression. They believe that we are mistaken in our level of analysis.

I have chosen pornography as an example because its discourse is the most symptomatic and the most demonstrative of the violence which is done to us through discourses, as well as in the society at large. There is nothing abstract about the power that sciences and theories have to act materially and actually upon our bodies and our minds, even if the discourse that produces it is abstract. It is one of the forms of domination, its very expression. I would say, rather, one of its exercises. All of the oppressed know this power and have had to deal with it. It is the one which says: you do not have the right to speech because your discourse is not scientific and not theoretical, you are on the wrong level of analysis, you are confusing discourse and reality, your discourse is naive, you misunderstand this or that science.

If the discourse of modern theoretical systems and social science exert a power upon us, it is because it works with concepts which closely touch us. In spite of the historic advent of the lesbian, feminist, and gay liberation movements, whose proceedings have already upset the philosophical and political categories of the discourses of the social sciences, their categories (thus brutally put into question) are nevertheless utilized without examination by contemporary science. They function like primitive concepts in a conglomerate of all kinds of disciplines, theories, and current ideas that I will call the straight mind. (See *The Savage Mind* by Claude Lévi-Strauss.) They concern "woman," "man," "sex," "difference," and all of the series of concepts which bear this mark, including such concepts as "history," "culture," and the "real." And although it has been accepted in recent years that there is no such thing as nature, that everything is culture, there remains within that culture a core of nature which resists examination, a relationship excluded from the social in the analysis — a relationship whose characteristic is ineluctability in culture, as well as in nature, and which is the heterosexual relationship. I will call it the obligatory social relationship between "man" and "woman." (Here I refer to Ti-Grace Atkinson and her analysis of sexual intercourse as an institution.[6]) With its ineluctability as knowledge, as an obvious principle, as a given prior to any science, the straight mind develops a totalizing interpretation of history, social reality, culture, language, and all the subjective phenomena at the same time. I can only underline the oppressive character that the straight mind is clothed in in its tendency to immediately universalize its production of concepts into general laws which claim to hold true for all societies, all epochs, all individuals. Thus one speaks of *the* exchange of women, *the* difference between the sexes, *the* symbolic order, *the* Unconscious, Desire, *Jouissance,* Culture,

History, giving an absolute meaning to these concepts when they are only categories founded upon heterosexuality, or thought which produces the difference between the sexes as a political and philosophical dogma.

The consequence of this tendency toward universality is that the straight mind cannot conceive of a culture, a society where heterosexuality would not order not only all human relationships but also its very production of concepts and all the processes which escape consciousness, as well. Additionally, these unconscious processes are historically more and more imperative in what they teach us about ourselves through the instrumentality of specialists. The rhetoric which expresses them (and whose seduction I do not underestimate) envelops itself in myths, resorts to enigma, proceeds by accumulating metaphors, and its function is to poeticize the obligatory character of the "you-will-be-straight-or-you-will-not-be."

In this thought, to reject the obligation of coitus and the institutions that this obligation has produced as necessary for the constitution of a society, is simply an impossibility, since to do this would mean to reject the possibility of the constitution of the other and to reject the "symbolic order," to make the constitution of meaning impossible, without which no one can maintain an internal coherence. Thus lesbianism, homosexuality, and the societies that we form cannot be thought of or spoken of, even though they have always existed. Thus, the straight mind continues to affirm that incest, and not homosexuality, represents its major interdiction. Thus, when thought by the straight mind, homosexuality is nothing but heterosexuality.

Yes, straight society is based on the necessity of the different/other at every level. It cannot work economically, symbolically,

Freud

linguistically, or politically without this concept. This necessity of the different/other is an ontological one for the whole conglomerate of sciences and disciplines that I call the straight mind. But what is the different/other if not the dominated? For heterosexual society is the society which not only oppresses lesbians and gay men, it oppresses many different/others, it oppresses all women and many categories of men, all those who are in the position of the dominated. To constitute a difference and to control it is an "act of power, since it is essentially a normative act. Everybody tries to show the other as different. But not everybody succeeds in doing so. One has to be socially dominant to succeed in it."[7]

For example, the concept of difference between the sexes ontologically constitutes women into different/others. Men are not different, whites are not different, nor are the masters. But the blacks, as well as the slaves, are. This ontological characteristic of the difference between the sexes affects all the concepts which are part of the same conglomerate. But for us there is no such thing as being-woman or being-man. "Man" and "woman" are political concepts of opposition, and the copula which dialectically unites them is, at the same time, the one which abolishes them.[8] It is the class struggle between women and men which will abolish men and women.[9] The concept of difference has nothing ontological about it. It is only the way that the masters interpret a historical situation of domination. The function of difference is to mask at every level the conflicts of interest, including ideological ones.

In other words, for us, this means there cannot any longer be women and men, and that as classes and categories of thought or language they have to disappear, politically, economically, ideologically. If we, as lesbians and gay men, continue to speak of ourselves and to conceive of ourselves as women and as men, we are instrumental in maintaining heterosexuality. I am sure that an economic and political transformation will not dedramatize these categories of language. Can we redeem *slave?* Can we redeem *nigger, negress?* How is *woman* different? Will we continue to write *white, master, man?* The transformation of economic relationships will not suffice. We must produce a political transformation of the key concepts, that is of the concepts which are strategic for us. For there is another order of materiality, that of language, and language is worked upon from within by these strategic concepts. It is at the same time tightly connected to the political field, where everything that concerns language, science and thought refers to the person as subjectivity and to her/his relationship to society. And we cannot leave this within the power of the straight mind or the thought of domination.

If among all the productions of the straight mind I especially challenge the models of the Structural Unconscious, it is because: at the moment in history when the domination of social groups can no longer appear as a logical necessity to the dominated, because they revolt, because they question the differences, Lévi-Strauss, Lacan, and their epigones call upon necessities which escape the control of consciousness and therefore the responsibility of individuals.

psychoanalysts they pretend nothing can be done

They call upon unconscious processes, for example, which require the exchange of women as a necessary condition for every society. According to them, that is what the unconscious tells us with authority, and the symbolic order, without which there is no meaning, no language, no society, depends on it. But what does women being exchanged mean if not that they are dominated? No wonder then that there is only one Unconscious, and that it is heterosexual. It is an Unconscious which looks too consciously after the interests of the masters[10] in whom it lives for them to be dispossessed of their concepts so easily. Besides, domination is denied; there is no slavery of women, there is difference. To which I will answer with this statement made by a Rumanian peasant at a public meeting in 1848: "Why do the gentlemen say it was not slavery, for we know it to have been slavery, this sorrow that we have sorrowed." Yes, we know it, and this science of oppression cannot be taken away from us.

It is from this science that we must track down the "what-goes-without-saying" heterosexual, and (I paraphrase the early Roland Barthes) we must not bear "seeing Nature and History confused at every turn."[11] We must make it brutally apparent that psychoanalysis after Freud and particularly Lacan have rigidly turned their concepts into myths — Difference, Desire, the Name-of-the-father, etc. They have even "over-mythified" the myths, an operation that was necessary for them in order to systematically heterosexualize that personal dimension which suddenly emerged through the dominated individuals into the historical field, particularly through women, who started their struggle almost two centuries ago. And it has been done systematically, in a concert of interdisciplinarity, never more harmonious than since the heterosexual myths started to circulate with ease from one formal system to another, like sure values that can be invested in anthropology as well as in psychoanalysis and in all the social sciences.

This ensemble of heterosexual myths is a system of signs which uses figures of speech, and thus it can be politically studied from within the science of our oppression; "for-we-know-it-to-have-been-slavery" is the dynamic which introduces the diachronism of history into the fixed discourse of eternal essences. This undertaking should somehow be a political semiology, although with "this sorrow that we have sorrowed" we work also at the level of language/manifesto, of language/action, that which transforms, that which makes history.

In the meantime, in the systems that seemed so eternal and universal that laws could be extracted from them, laws that could be stuffed into computers, and in any case for the moment stuffed into the unconscious machinery, in these systems, thanks to our action and our language, shifts are happening. Such a model, as for example, the exchange of women, reengulfs history in so violent and brutal a way that the whole system, which was believed to be formal, topples over into another dimension of knowledge. This dimension of history belongs to us, since somehow we have been designated, and since, as Lévi-Strauss said, we talk, let us say that we break off the heterosexual contract.

So, this is what lesbians say everywhere in this country and in some others, if not with theories at least through their social practice, whose repercussions upon straight culture and society are still unenvisionable. An anthropologist might say that we have to wait for fifty years. Yes, if one wants to universalize the functioning of these societies and make their invariants appear. Meanwhile the straight concepts are undermined. What is woman? Panic, general alarm for an active defense. Frankly, it is a problem that the lesbians do not have because of a change of perspective, and it would be incorrect to say that lesbians associate, make love, live with women, for "woman" has meaning only in heterosexual systems of thought and heterosexual economic systems. Lesbians are not women.

What then constitutes lesbian identity?

ON THE SOCIAL CONTRACT

1989

I have undertaken a difficult task, which is to measure and re-
evaluate the notion of the social contract, taken as a notion of
political philosophy. A notion born with the seventeenth and
eighteenth centuries, it is also the title of a book by J.-J. Rousseau.[1] Marx and Engels criticized it because it was not relevant
in terms of class struggle and therefore did not concern the proletariat. In *The German Ideology* they explain that the proletarian class, due to its relation to production and labor, can only
confront the social order as an ensemble, as a whole, and that
it has no choice but to destroy the state. In their opinion the
term "social contract," which implies a notion of individual
choice and of voluntary association, could possibly be applied
to the serfs. For in the course of several centuries they liberated
themselves one by one, running away from the land to which
they belonged. And it is also one by one that the serfs associated
to form cities, hence their name, *bourgeois* (people who have
formed a bourg).[2] (It seems that as soon as Rousseau developed
the idea of the social contract as far as it has ever been developed, history outdated it — but not before some of his propositions were adopted without amendment by the French Revolutionary Assembly.)

I have always thought that women are a class structured very much as was the class of serfs. I see now that they can tear themselves away from the heterosexual order only by running away one by one. This explains my concern for a preindustrial notion such as the social contract. For the structure of our class in terms of the whole world is feudal in essence, maintaining side by side and in the same persons forms of production and of exploitation that are at the same time capitalist and precapitalist.[3]

In broad terms that is one aspect of my task. Another aspect has to do with language. For to a writer language offers a very concrete matter to grasp hold of. It seems to me that the first, the permanent, and the final social contract is language. The basic agreement between human beings, indeed what makes them human and makes them social, is language. The story of the Tower of Babel is a perfect illustration of what happens when the agreement breaks down.

Since I have used the term "heterosexual contract"[4] several times in my past writings, as well as referring to the "social contract as heterosexual," it has become my task to reflect on the notion of the social contract. Why is this notion so compelling even though it has supposedly been given up by modern science and history? Why does it reverberate here and now far from its initial momentum in the Enlightenment of the eighteenth century? Why at the same time did I urge vehemently that we should break off the heterosexual social contract? The general question of the social contract in so far as it encompasses all human activity, thought, and relations is a philosophical question always present as long as "humankind [that] was born free . . . is everywhere in chains," to quote Rousseau. Its promise of being achieved for the good of all and of everyone can still be the object of a philosophical examination, and, since it has not been fulfilled by history, it retains its utopian dimension. Thus formulated in its general aspect, the question extends to all humankind. Now when I say let us break off the heterosexual contract per se, I designate the group "women." But I did not mean that we must break off the social contract per se, because that would be absurd. For we must break it off as heterosexual. Leaning upon a philosophical examination of what a well-established social contract could do for us, I want to confront the historical conditions and conflicts that can lead us to end the obligations that bind us without our consent while we are not enjoying a reciprocal commitment that would be the necessary condition for our freedom, to paraphrase Rousseau.

The question of the social contract in the very terms of Jean-Jacques Rousseau is far from being obsolete, for, in what concerns its philosophical dimension, it was never developed further. The question of the sexes, which itself delineated very narrowly the general design of society, if approached from a philosophical point of view, encompasses and embodies the general idea of social contract. There are historical reasons as well to resuscitate the notion of social contract that have to do with the structures of the groups of sex and their particular situation among the relations of production and social intercourse.

The main approach to the notion of social contract must be a philosophical one, in the sense that a philosophical point of view allows the possibility of synthesis, in contrast to the divided point of view of the social sciences.[5] And indeed "social contract" is a notion of political philosophy, the abstract idea that there is a pact, a compact, an agreement between individuals and the social order. The idea came into existence with the English philosophers of the seventeenth century, Thomas Hobbes (*Leviathan*) and John Locke (*Treatise of Government*), and the French philosophers of the Enlightenment, chiefly Rousseau. The appearance of the idea according to the historians of ideas was a result of the questioning of the old medieval theories concerning the state. According to these theories the state could only be a theocracy, since all authority emanates from God, and kings rule to achieve a divine order, as they are kings by divine right.

Philosophers long before the "social contract" came into existence had their attention fixed on the composition of society. The philosophers were apprentice legislators and rulers. They thought about the best government and the ideal city. Political questions were then asked, taught, and discussed as philosophical questions, politics being a branch of philosophy. There was a narrow margin between their elaborations and utopia, since many of them had been confronted with practical problems: Plato was called to the court of Sicily by Denys the tyrant. Then later on he taught and educated his nephew who was to become a king. Aristotle was the preceptor of Alexander. Plotinus was given the means by another tyrant to construct and create the ideal city, a long-time object of speculation and hope. Being caught in such a close connection between speculation and ruling, the philosophers must have known that there was a utopian limit to their creations. I imagine it thus, because of the trials they had to go through in reality when they approached too closely to the throne. In the ninth book of *The Republic* Socrates and Glaucon discuss the perfect city and its ideal form:

GLAUCON: "But the city whose foundation we have been describing has its being only in words; there is no spot on earth where it exists."

SOCRATES: "No; but it is laid up in heaven as a pattern for him who wills to see, and seeing, to found that city in himself. Whether it exists anywhere, or ever will exist, is no matter."

No wonder then that Rousseau in the opening of *The Social Contract* addresses the reader thus: "I may be asked whether I am a prince or a legislator that I should be writing about politics." And Rousseau, who wanted to distance himself from those he called with contempt the philosophers, says; "I answer no." But several of his propositions were adopted directly, without transformation by the Revolutionary Assembly. These direct connections of the philosophers to tyrants, kings, and political assemblies may seem to us to belong to the domain of the marvelous. However, we can remember how recently President Kennedy asked the members of his staff to prepare a report on the situation of women. And the initiative of these women gave birth to one of the first detachments of the women's liberation movement, instigated by persons all very near to the "throne."

But if, at the start of politics, a philosopher like Aristotle was aware that society was a "combination," an "association," a "coming together," it was not a voluntary association. For Aristotle, society could never be established with the agreement of its members and for their best good, but as the result of a "*coup de force*," an imposition of the clever ones upon the bodily strong, but feeble-minded ones. Indeed for Aristotle the strong, the powerful, are those with intelligence, while those possessing bodily strength fall into the category of the weak. In his words: "Essential is the combination of ruler and ruled, the purpose of their coming together being their common safety. For he that can by his intelligence foresee things needed is by nature ruler and master; while he whose bodily strength enables him to perform them is by nature a slave, one of those who are ruled. Thus there is a common interest uniting master and slave."[6] Hobbes and Locke use the terms *covenant, compact, agreement,* and after them so does Rousseau, while he emphasizes a term much more politically rigorous: *the social contract.*

Covenant, compact, agreement refer to an initial covenant establishing once and for all the binding of people together. According to Rousseau the social contract is the sum of fundamental conventions which "even though they might never have been formally enunciated are nevertheless implied by living in society." Clearly, in what Rousseau says, it is the real present existence of the social contract that is particularly stimulating for me — whatever its origin, it exists here and now, and as such it is apt to be understood and acted upon. Each contractor has to reaffirm the contract in new terms for the contract to be in existence.

Only then does it become an instrumental notion in the sense that the contractors are reminded by the term itself that they should reexamine their conditions. Society was not made once and for all. The social contract will yield to our action, to our words. Even if we say no more than Rousseau: "I was born the citizen of a free state and the very right to vote imposes on me the duty to instruct myself in public affairs, however little influence my voice may have in them."

Rousseau is the first philosopher who does not take it for granted that, if there is such a thing as a social contract, its nerve is "might is right" (and under other phraseology belonging to the conscious or the unconscious order, modern historians and anthropologists seem to yield to the inevitability of this principle in society in the name of science). Nothing is more enjoyable than his sarcasm about the "right of the strongest," which he shows to be a contradiction in terms. In *The Social Contract* he says:

The strongest man is never strong enough to be master all the time. . . . The "right of the strongest" — a "right" that sounds like something intended ironically, but is actually laid down as a principle. . . . To yield to force is an act of necessity not of will; it is at best an act of prudence. In what sense can it be a moral duty? . . . Once might is made to be right, cause and effect are reversed. . . . But, what can be the validity of a right which perishes with the force on which it rests? If force compels obedience, there is no need to invoke a duty to obey, and if force ceases to compel obedience, there is no longer any obligation. Thus the word "right" adds nothing to what is said by "force," it is meaningless.

I come back to the historical situation women are in, and which makes it at least appropriate for them to reflect upon what has affected their existence without their agreement. I am not a prince, I am not a legislator, but an active member of society. I consider it my duty to examine the set of rules, obligations, and constraints this society has placed upon me, if rules and obligations provide me with the freedom I would not find in nature, or if it is not the case to say with Rousseau that society has taken us in, in these terms: "I make a covenant with you which is wholly at your expense and wholly to my advantage; I will respect it so long as I please and you should respect it as long as I wish." (The term is used here rhetorically, since everybody knows that there is no way out of society.) But whether we want it or not, we are living in society here and now, and proof is given that we say yes to the social bond when we conform to the conventions and rules that were never formally enunciated but that nevertheless everybody knows and applies like magic.

Proof is given that we say yes to the social bond when we talk a common language as we do now. Most people would not use the term "social contract" to describe their situation within the social order. However, they would agree that there are a certain number of acts and things one "must do." *Outlaw* and *mad* are the names for those who refuse to go by the rules and conventions, as well as for those who refuse to or cannot speak the common language. And this is what interests me when I talk of the social contract: precisely the rules and conventions that have never been formally enunciated, the rules and conventions that go without saying for the scientific mind as well as for the common people, that which for them obviously makes life possible, exactly as one must have two legs and two arms, or one must breathe to live. Being tied together by a social link, we can consider that each and every one of us stands within the social contract — the social contract being then the fact of having come together, of being together, of living as social beings. This notion is relevant for the philosophical mind, even if it is not instrumental anymore for the scientific mind, through the established fact that we live, function, talk, work, marry together. Indeed the conventions and the language show on a dotted line the bulk of the social contract — which consists in living in heterosexuality. For to live in society is to live in heterosexuality. In fact, in my mind social contract and heterosexuality are two superimposable notions.

The social contract I am talking about is heterosexuality.

The problem I am facing in trying to define the social contract is the same kind of problem I have when I try to define what heterosexuality is. I confront a nonexistent object, a fetish, an ideological form which cannot be grasped in reality, except through its effects, whose existence lies in the mind of people, but in a way that affects their whole life, the way they act, the way they move, the way they think. So we are dealing with an object both imaginary and real. If I try to look at the dotted line that delineates the bulk of the social contract, it moves, it shifts, and sometimes it produces something visible, and sometimes it disappears altogether. It looks like the Möbius strip. Now I see this, now I see something quite different. But this Möbius strip is fake, because only one aspect of the optical effect appears distinctly and massively, and that is heterosexuality. Homosexuality appears like a ghost only dimly and sometimes not at all.

Appears 2 B 2 realitys but only 1 - Hetero - in our society

What then is heterosexuality? As a term it was created as a counterpart of homosexuality at the beginning of this century. So much for the extent of its "it-goes-without-saying." Jurists would not call it an institution, or, in other words, heterosexuality as an institution has no juridic existence (marriage's jurisdiction in French legislation does not even mention that the partners of the contract must be of different sexes). Anthropologists, ethnologists, sociologists would come to take it for an institution, but as an unwritten, unspoken one. For they assume a quality of already-there, due to something exterior to a social order, of two groups: men and women. For them, men are social beings, women are natural beings. I compare it to the approach of psychoanalysts when they assume there is a preoedipal relation of the child to the mother, a presocial relation which in spite of its importance for humankind does not emerge from history. This view has for them the advantage in terms of the social contract of doing away with the problem of origins. They believe that they are dealing with a diachrony instead of a synchrony.

So does Lévi-Strauss with his famous notion of the exchange of women. He believes that he deals with invariants. He and all the social scientists who do not see the problem I am trying to underline would of course never talk in terms of "social contract." It is indeed much simpler to take what I call "social contract" in terms of status quo, that is, in terms of something that *has* not changed, *will* not change. Thus we have in their literature these words: *fathers, mothers, brothers, sisters,* etc., whose relations can be studied as though they had to go on as such for ever.

Aristotle was much more cynical when he stated in *The Politics* that things *must be:* "The first point is that those which are ineffective without each other *must be* united in a pair. For example, the union of male and female" (emphasis added). Notice that this point of the necessity of heterosexuality is the first point of *The Politics.* And notice also that the second example of "those . . . which *must be* united as a pair" is found in "the combination of ruler and ruled." From that time on, male and female, the heterosexual relationship, has been the parameter of all hierarchical relations. It is almost useless to underline that it is only the dominated members of the pair that are "ineffective" by themselves. For "ruler" and "male" go very well without their counterpart.

Now I return to Lévi-Strauss, for I am not going to pass by the idea of the exchange of women, which until now has been so favored by feminist theoreticians. And not by chance, since with this theory we have revealed the whole plot, the whole conspiracy, of fathers, brothers, husbands against half of humankind. For the masters, slaves are certainly more transient than women in the use one can have of them. Women, "the slaves of the poor" as Aristotle called them, are always there at hand; they are the valuables that make life worthwhile according to Lévi-Strauss (Aristotle would have said it not very differently: they make for the "good life"). When Lévi-Strauss described what the exchange of women is and how it works, he was obviously drawing for us the broad lines of the social contract, but a social contract from which women are excluded, a social contract between men. Each time the exchange takes place it confirms between men a contract of appropriation of all women. For Lévi-Strauss, society cannot function or exist without this exchange. By showing it he exposes heterosexuality as not only an institution but as *the* social contract, as a political regime. (You have noticed that sexual pleasure and sexual modes are not the question here.) Lévi-Strauss answers the charges of antifeminism which such a theory rewarded him with. And, although he conceded that women could not be completely superimposable with the signs of language with which he compared them in terms of exchange, he had no reason to worry about the shocking effect such a theory can have upon women, any more than Aristotle had when he defined the necessity of the slaves in the social order, because a scientific mind must not be embarrassed and shy when dealing with crude reality. And this is crude reality indeed. There cannot be any fear of a rebellion in the case of women. Even better, they have been convinced that they want what they are forced to do and that they are part of the contract of society that excludes them. Because even if they, if we, do not consent, we cannot think outside of the mental categories of heterosexuality. Heterosexuality is always already there within all mental categories. It has sneaked into dialectical thought (or thought of differences) as its main category. For even abstract philosophical categories act upon the real as social. Language casts sheaves of reality upon the social body, stamping it and violently shaping it. For example, the bodies of social actors are fashioned by abstract language (as well as by nonabstract languages). For there is a plasticity of the real to language.

Thus heterosexuality, whose characteristics appear and then disappear when the mind tries to grasp it, is visible and obvious in the categories of the heterosexual contract. One of them which I tried to deconstruct in a short essay [included in this volume] is the category of sex. And it is clear that with it we deal with a political category. A category which when put flatly makes us understand the terms of the social contract for women. I quote from "The Category of Sex" (with slightly revised wording):

The perenniality of the sexes and the perenniality of slaves and masters proceed from the same belief. And as there are no slaves without masters, there are no women without men. . . .

The category of sex is the political category that founds society as heterosexual. As such it does not concern being but relationships (for women and men are the result of relationships), although the two aspects are always confused when they are discussed. The category of sex is the one that rules as "natural" the relation that is at the base of (heterosexual) society and through which half of the population, women, are "heterosexualized." . . .

Its main category, the category of *sex, works specifically, as "black" does, through an operation of reduction, by taking the part for the whole, a part (color, sex) through which the whole human being has to pass as through a screen.* (Emphasis added)

When Adrienne Rich said "heterosexuality is compulsory," it was a step forward in the comprehension of the kind of social contract we are dealing with. Nicole-Claude Mathieu, a French anthropologist, in a remarkable essay on consciousness, made it clear that it is not because we remain silent that we consent.[7]

And how can we consent to a social contract that reduces us, by obligation, to sexual beings meaningful only through their reproductive activities or, to quote the French writer Jean Paulhan, to beings in whom everything, even their minds, is sex?[8]

In conclusion I will say that only by running away from their class can women achieve the social contract (that is, a new one), even if they have to do it like the fugitive serfs, one by one. We are doing it. Lesbians are runaways, fugitive slaves; runaway wives are the same case, and they exist in all countries, because the political regime of heterosexuality represents all cultures. So that breaking off the heterosexual social contract is a necessity for those who do not consent to it. For if there is something real in the ideas of Rousseau, it is that we can form "voluntary associations" here and now, and here and now reformulate the social contract as a new one, although we are not princes or legislators. Is this mere utopia? Then I will stay with Socrates's view and also Glaucon's: If ultimately we are denied a new social order, which therefore can exist only in words, I will find it in myself.

HOMO SUM

1990

Homo sum; humani nihil a me alienum puto.
(Man am I; nothing human is alien to me.)
— Terence, *Heauton Timoroumenos*, 25 (*The Self-Tormentor*)

All of us have an abstract idea of what being "human" means, even if what we mean when we say "human" is still potential and virtual, has not yet been actualized. For indeed, for all its pretension to being universal, what has been until now considered "human" in our Western philosophy concerns only a small fringe of people: white men, proprietors of the means of production, along with the philosophers who theorized their point of view as the only and exclusively possible one. This is the reason why when we consider abstractly, from a philosophical point of view, the potentiality and virtuality of humanness, we need to do it, to see clearly, from an oblique point of view. Thus, being a lesbian, standing at the outposts of the human (of humankind) represents historically and paradoxically the most human point of view. This idea that from an extreme point of view one can criticize and modify the thought and the structures of society at large is not a new one. We owe it to Robespierre and Saint-Just.

Marx and Engels in their *German Ideology* extended the idea by affirming the necessity for the most radical groups to show their point of view and their interests as general and universal, a stand that touches both the practical and philosophical (political) points of view.

The situation of lesbians here and now in society, whether they know it or not, is located philosophically (politically) beyond the categories of sex. Practically they have run away from their class (the class of women), even if only partially and precariously.

It is from this cultural and practical site, both extremely vulnerable and crucial, that I will raise the question of dialectics.

There is, on one side, the whole world in its massive assumption, its massive affirmation of heterosexuality as a must-be, and on the other side, there is only the dim, fugitive, sometimes illuminating and striking vision of heterosexuality as a trap, as a forced political regime, that is, with the possibility of escaping it as a fact.

Our political thought has been for more than a century shaped by dialectics. Those of us who have discovered dialectical thought through its most modern form, the Marxian and Engelsian one, that is, the producer of the theory of class struggle, had, in order to understand its mechanism, to refer to Hegel, particularly if they needed to comprehend the reversal which Marx and Engels inflicted on Hegel's dialectics. That is, briefly, a dynamization of the essentialist categories of Hegel, a transport from metaphysics to politics (to show that in the political and social field metaphysical terms had to be interpreted in terms of conflicts, and not anymore in terms of essential oppositions, and to show that the conflicts could be overcome and the categories of opposition reconciled).

A remark here: Marx and Engels, in summarizing all the social oppositions in terms of class struggle and class struggle only, reduced all the conflicts under two terms. This was an operation of reduction which did away with a series of conflicts that could be subsumed under the appellation of "capital's anachronisms." Racism, antisemitism and sexism have been hit by the Marxian reduction. The theory of conflict that they originated could be expressed by a paradigm that crossed all the Marxist "classes." They could not be interpreted exclusively in economic terms: that is, in terms of the bare appropriation of surplus value in a sociological context where all are equal in rights, but where the capitalists because they possess the means of production can appropriate most of the workers' production and work as far as it produces a value that is exchangeable in terms of money and the market. Every conflict whose forms could not be flattened to the two terms of the class struggle was supposed to be solved after the proletarian class assumed power.

We know that historically the theory of the class struggle did not win, and the world is still divided into capitalists (owners of the means of production) and workers (providers of work and labor strength and producers of surplus value). The consequence of the failure of the proletarian class to change the social relationships in all countries leads us to a dead end. In terms of dialectics the result is a freezing of the Marxian dynamics, the return to a metaphysical thought and the superimposition of essentialist terms onto the terms that were to be transformed through Marxian dialectics. In other words, we are still facing a capitalist versus a proletarian class, but this time, as though they had been struck by the wand of the Sleeping Beauty fairy, they are here to stay, they are struck by the coin of fate, immobilized, changed into essential terms, emptied of the dynamic relationship that could transform them.

For my purpose here there is no need to go into a deep reexamination of the Marxian approach, except to say in terms of the world equilibrium that what Marx called the anachronisms of capital, of the industrial world, cover up a mass of different people, half of humankind in the persons of women, the colonized, the third world and *le quart monde*,[1] and the peasants in the industrial world. Lenin and Mao Zedong had to face the problem with their masses early in the century.

From a lesbian political philosophical point of view, when one reflects on women's situation in history, one needs to interrogate dialectics further back than Hegelian dialectics, back to its originating locus; that is, one needs to go back to Aristotle and Plato to comprehend how the categories of opposition that have shaped us were born.

Of the first Greek philosophers, some were materialists and all were monists, which means that they did not see any division in Being, Being as being was one. According to Aristotle, we owe to the Pythagorean school the division in the process of thought and therefore in the thought of Being. Then, instead of thinking in terms of unity, philosophers introduced duality in thought, in the process of reasoning.

Consider the first table of opposites which history has handed down to us, as it has been recorded by Aristotle (*Metaphysics*, Book I, 5, 6):

Limited	Unlimited
Odd	Even
One	Many
Right	Left

Male	Female
Rest	Motion
Straight	Curved
Light	Dark
Good	Bad
Square	Oblong

We may observe that

right	left
male	female
light	dark
good	bad

are terms of judgment and evaluation, ethical concepts, that are foreign to the series from which I extracted them. The first series is a technical, instrumental series corresponding to a division needed by the tool for which it was created (a kind of carpenter's square called a gnomon). Since Pythagoras and the members of his school were mathematicians, one can comprehend their series. The second series is heterogeneous to the first one. So it so happens that as soon as the precious conceptual tools resting on division (variations, comparisons, differences) were created, they were immediately (or almost immediately by the successors of the school of Pythagoras) turned into a means of creating metaphysical and moral differentiation in Being.

There is then with Aristotle a displacement, a jump in the comprehension of these concepts, which he used for his historical approach to philosophy and what he called metaphysics. From being practical concepts they became abstract ones. From terms whose function had been to sort out, to classify, to make measurement possible (in itself a work of genius) they were translated into a metaphysical dimension, and pretty soon they got totally dissociated from their context. Furthermore, the evaluative and ethical terms (right, male, light, good) of the tabulation of opposites, as used within the metaphysical interpretation of Aristotle (and Plato), modified the meaning of technical terms like "One." Everything that was "good" belonged to the series of the One (as Being). Everything that was "many" (different) belonged to the series of the "bad," assimilated to nonbeing, to unrest, to everything that questions what is good. Thus we left the domain of deduction to enter the domain of interpretation.

In the dialectical field created by Plato and Aristotle we find a series of oppositions inspired by the first mathematical tabulation, but distorted. Thus under the series of the "One" (the absolute being nondivided, divinity itself) we have "male" (and "light") that were from then on never dislodged from their dominant position. Under the other series appear the unrestful: the common people, the females, the "slaves of the poor," the "dark" (barbarians who cannot distinguish between slaves and women), all reduced to the parameter of non-Being. For Being is being good, male, straight, one, in other words, godlike, while non-Being is being anything else (many), female: it means discord, unrest, dark, and bad. (See Aristotle's *Politics*.)

Plato played with the terms One and the Same (as being God and the Good) and the Other (which is not the same as God which is non-Being, bad). Thus dialectics operates on a series of oppositions that basically have a metaphysical connotation: Being or non-Being. From our point of view, Hegel, in his dialectics of master versus slave, does not proceed very differently. Marx himself, although trying to historicize the oppositions into conflicts (social ones, practical ones), was a prisoner of the metaphysical series, of the dialectical series. Bourgeoisie is on the side of the One, of Being; Proletariat is on the side of the Other, the non-Being.

Thus the need, the necessity of questioning dialectics consists for us in the "dialecticizing" of dialectics, questioning it in relation to its terms or opposition as principles and also in its functioning. For if in the history of philosophy there was a jump from deduction to interpretation and contradiction, or, in other words, if from mathematical and instrumental categories we jumped to the normative and metaphysical categories, shouldn't we call attention to it?

Shouldn't we mention that the paradigm to which female, dark, bad, and unrest belong has also been augmented by slave, Other, different? Every philosopher of our modern age, including the linguists, the psychoanalysts, the anthropologists, will tell us that without these precise categories of opposition (of difference), one cannot reason or think or, even better, that outside of them meaning cannot shape itself, there is an impossibility of meaning as outside of society, in the asocial.

Certainly Marx intended to turn Hegel's dialectics upside down. The step forward for Marx was to show that dialectical categories such as the One and the Other, Master and Slave, were not there to stay and had nothing metaphysical or essential about them, but had to be read and understood in historical terms. With this gesture he was reestablishing the link between philosophy and politics. Thus the categories which are today called so solemnly categories of Difference (belonging to what I call the thought of Difference) were for Marx conflictual categories — categories of social conflicts — which throughout the class struggle were supposed to destroy each other. And, as it had to happen in such a struggle, in destroying (abolishing) the

One, the Other was also going to destroy (abolish) itself. For as soon as the proletariat constituted itself as an economic class, it had to destroy itself as well as the bourgeoisie. The process of destruction consists in a double movement: destroying itself as a class (otherwise the bourgeoisie keeps the power) and destroying itself as a philosophical category (the category of the Other), for staying mentally in the category of the Other (of the slave) would mean a nonresolution in terms of Marxian dialectics. The resolution then tends toward a philosophical reevaluation of the two conflictual terms, which as soon as it makes clear that there is an economic force where there was before a nonforce (a nothing), this force has to deny itself on the side of the Other (slave) and to take over on the side of the One (master), but only to abolish both orders, thus reconciling them to make them the same and only one.

What has happened in history throughout the revolutions which we have known is that the Other (a category of others) has substituted itself for the One, keeping under it huge groups of oppressed peoples that would in turn become the Other of the ex-others, become by then the One. This happened already (before Marx) with the French Revolution, which could not deal very well with the questions of slavery and did not deal at all with the questions of women (Woman, the eternal Other). To dialecticize dialectics seems to me to question what will really happen to the question of humanness once all categories of others will be transferred onto the side of the One, of Being, of the Subject. Will there be no transformation? For example, in terms of language will we be able to keep the terms "humanity," "human," "man," "*l'homme*," "*homo*," even though all these terms in the abstract mean first the human being without distinction of sex)? Shall we keep these terms after they have been appropriated for so long by the dominant group (men over women) and after they have been used to mean both abstractly and concretely humanity as male? Mankind: Malekind. In other words a philosophical and political abuse.

This necessary transformation (a dialectical operation) was not dealt with by Marx and Engels. They were dealing (as usual with revolutions) with a substitution. For a good reason: because they were writing about the issue *before* the event of a proletarian revolution and could not determine before the fact what would happen. For a bad reason: the bearers of the Universal, of the General, of the Human, of the One, was the bourgeois class (see *The Communist Manifesto*), the yeast of history, the only class able to go beyond the national bounds. The proletarian class, although the climbing one, had stayed for them at the stage of limbo, a mass of ghosts that needed the direction of the Communist Party (its members themselves mostly bourgeois) to subsist and fight.

Thus perished our most perfect model of dialectics, of materialist dialectics, because the dice were loaded: the Other from the start was condemned to stay in the place where it was to be found at first in the relationship, that is, *essentially* in the Other's place, since the agency that was to achieve the class transformation (that is, to break down the categories of the One and the Other, and to turn them into something else) belonged to the parameter of the One, that is, to the bourgeoisie itself.

When it was upon the bourgeoisie by the means of its revolutionary fraction that Marxian dialectics imposed the demand of fighting itself and of reducing itself to nothing, through the reduction of both classes, could we expect them to do it? For the representatives of the Communist Party mostly did belong, did come from, the bourgeois class through its intellectuals.

This issue, even more crucial as far as women and men are concerned, is still in its infancy, barely questioned. It is scarcely possible to position women in relation to men. Who is actually reasonable enough to conceive that it is necessary, or that it will be necessary to destroy these categories as categories and to end the domination of the "One" over the Other? Which is not to say to substitute women for men (the Other for the One).

Actually, as of old, men are on one side and women are on the other. The "Ones" dominate and possess everything, including women, the others are dominated and appropriated. What I believe in such a situation is that at the level of philosophy and politics women should do without the privilege of being different and above all never formulate this imposition of being different (relegated to the category of the Other) as a "right to be different," or never abandon themselves to the "pride of being different." Since politically and economically the matter seems to be very slow to get settled, it seems to me that philosophically one can be helped by the process of abstraction.

In the abstract, mankind, Man, is everybody — the Other, whatever its kind, is included. Once the possibility of abstraction becomes a fact among human beings, there are at this level certain facts that can be made clear.

There is no need when coming under the parameters of the oppressed to follow the Marxian design and to wait until the "final victory" to declare that the oppressed are human as well as the dominators, that women are human as well as men. Where *what does she mean by "universal" here?*

on for us to go on bearing with a series of ontological, and linguistic *entourloupettes*[2] under the
e do not have the power. It is part of our fight to
to say that one out of two men is a woman, that
belongs to us although we have been robbed and
his level as well as at the political and economic
oint maybe the dialectical method that I have ad-
can do very little for us. For abstractly, in the
ning, in the order of possibility and potentiality,
the Other cannot essentially *be* different from the
One, it *is* the Same, along the lines of what Voltaire called the
Sameness (*la "Mêmeté"*, a neologism he coined, never used in
French). No Thought of the Other or Thought of Difference
should be possible for us, for "nothing human is alien" to the
One or to the Other.

18 mc. sex contract

I believe we have not reached the end of what Reason can do
for us. And I do not want to deny my Cartesian cast of mind,
for I look back to the Enlightenment for the first glimmer of light
that history has given us. By now, however, Reason has been
turned into a representative of Order, Domination, Logocen-
trism. According to many of our contemporaries the only sal-
vation is in a tremendous exaltation of what they call alterity
under all of its forms: Jewish, Black, Red, Yellow, Female, Homosexual, Crazy. Far away from Reason (do they mean within
Folly?), "Different," and proud of being so.

Both the figureheads of the dominators and of the dominated
have adopted this point of view. Good is no more to be found
in the parameter of the One, of Male, of Light, but in the parameter of the Other, of Female, Darkness. So long live Unrea-

son, and let them be embarked anew in *la nef des fous,* the carnival, and so on. Never has the Other been magnified and celebrated to this extent. Other cultures, the mind of the Other, the Feminine brain, Feminine writing, and so on — we have during these last decades known everything as far as the Other is concerned.

I do not know who is going to profit from this abandonment of the oppressed to a trend that will make them more and more powerless, having lost the faculty of being subjects even before having gained it. I would say that we can renounce only what we have. And I would be glad to send the representatives of the dominators away back to back, whether they come from the party of the One or the party of the Other.

Naiveté, innocence, lack of doubt, certainty that everything is either black or white, certainty that when Reason is not sovereign then Unreason or Folly have the upper hand, belief that where there is Being there is also non-Being as a kind of refuse, and the most absurd of all things, the need and necessity in reaction to this evidence and these certainties to support and advocate, in contrast, a "right to Difference" (a right of difference) which by reversing everything corresponds to the Tweedledum and Tweedledee of Lewis Carroll — these are all the symptoms of what I have once called, out of exasperation, the straight mind. Sexes (gender), Difference between the sexes, man, woman, race, black, white, nature are at the core of its set of parameters. And they have shaped our concepts, our laws, our institutions, our history, our cultures.

They think they answer everything when they read metaphors in this double parameter, and to our analysis they object that there is a symbolic order, as though they were speaking of another dimension that would have nothing to do with domination. Alas for us, the symbolic order partakes of the same reality as the political and economic order. There is a continuum in their reality, a continuum where abstraction is imposed upon materiality and can shape the body as well as the mind of those it oppresses.

for Wed.

THE POINT OF VIEW:
UNIVERSAL OR PARTICULAR?

1980

I have gathered here a number of reflections on writing and language, which I wrote while translating Spillway *by Djuna Barnes, and which are related to Djuna Barnes's work and to my own work.*

I

That there is no "feminine writing" must be said at the outset, and one makes a mistake in using and giving currency to this expression. What is this "feminine" in "feminine writing"? It stands for Woman, thus merging a practice with a myth, the myth of Woman. "Woman" cannot be associated with writing because "Woman" is an imaginary formation and not a concrete reality; it is that old branding by the enemy now flourished like a tattered flag refound and won in battle. "Feminine writing" is the naturalizing metaphor of the brutal political fact of the domination of women, and as such it enlarges the apparatus under which "femininity" presents itself: that is, Difference, Specificity,

Female Body/Nature. Through its adjacent position, "writing" is captured by the metaphor in "feminine writing" and as a result fails to appear as work and a production process, since the words "writing" and "feminine" are combined in order to designate a sort of biological production peculiar to "Woman," a secretion natural to "Woman."

Thus, "feminine writing" amounts to saying that women do not belong to history, and that writing is not a material production. The (new) femininity, feminine writing, and the lauding of difference are the backlash of a political trend[1] very much concerned with the questioning of the categories of sex, those two great axes of categorization for philosophy and social science. As always happens, when something new appears, it is immediately interpreted and turned into its opposite. Feminine writing is like the household arts and cooking.

II

Gender is the linguistic index of the political opposition between the sexes. Gender is used here in the singular because indeed there are not two genders. There is only one: the feminine, the "masculine" not being a gender. For the masculine is not the masculine but the general.[2] The result is that there are the general and the feminine, or rather, the general and the mark of the feminine. It is this which makes Nathalie Sarraute say that she cannot use the feminine gender when she wants to generalize (and not particularize) what she is writing about. And since what is crucial for Sarraute is precisely abstracting from very concrete material, the use of the feminine is impossible when its presence distorts the meaning of her undertaking, due to the a priori analogy between feminine gender/sex/nature. Only the masculine as general is the abstract. The feminine is the concrete (sex in language). Djuna Barnes makes the experiment (and succeeds) by universalizing the feminine. (Like Proust she makes no difference in the way she describes male and female characters.) In doing so she succeeds in removing from the feminine gender its "smell of hatching," to use an expression of Baudelaire's about the poet Marceline Desbordes-Valmore. Djuna Barnes cancels out the genders by making them obsolete. I find it necessary to suppress them. That is the point of view of a lesbian.

III

The signifieds of nineteenth-century discourse have soaked the textual reality of our time to the saturation point. So, "'the genius of suspicion has appeared on the scene.'" So, "we have now entered upon an age of suspicion."[3] "Man" has lost ground to such an extent that he is barely acknowledged as the subject of discourse. Today they are asking: what is *the* subject? In the general debacle which has followed the calling of meaning into question, there is room for so-called minority writers to enter the privileged (battle) field of literature, where attempts at constitution of the subject confront each other. For since Proust we know that literary experimentation is a favored way to bring a subject to light. This experimentation is the ultimate subjective practice, a practice of the cognitive subject. Since Proust, the subject has never been the same, for throughout *Remembrance of Things Past* he made "homosexual" the axis of categorization from which to universalize. The minority subject is not self-centered as is the straight subject. Its extension into space could be described as being like Pascal's circle, whose center is everywhere and whose circumference is nowhere. This is what explains Djuna Barnes's angle of approach to her text — a constant shifting which, when the text is read, produces an effect comparable to what I call an out-of-the-corner-of-the-eye perception; the text works through fracturing. Word by word, the text bears the mark of that "estrangement" which Barnes describes with each of her characters.

I V

All minority writers (who are conscious of being so) enter into literature obliquely, if I may say so. The important problems in literature which preoccupy their contemporaries are framed by their perspective. They are as impassioned about problems of form as are straight writers, but also they cannot help but be stirred heart and soul by their subject — "that which calls for a hidden name," "that which dares not speak its name," that which they find everywhere although it is never written about. Writing a text which has homosexuality among its themes is a gamble. It is taking the risk that at every turn the formal element which is the theme will overdetermine the meaning, monopolize the whole meaning, against the intention of the author who wants above all to create a literary work. Thus the text which adopts such a theme sees one of its parts taken for the whole, one of the constituent elements of the text taken for the whole text, and the book become a symbol, a manifesto. When this happens, the text ceases to operate at the literary level; it is subjected to disregard, in the sense of ceasing to be regarded in relation to equivalent texts. It becomes a committed text with a social theme and it attracts attention to a social problem. When this happens to a text, it is diverted from its primary aim, which is to change the textual reality within which it is inscribed. In fact, by reason of its theme it is dismissed from that textual reality, it no longer has access to it, it is banned (often simply by the silent treatment or by failure to reprint), it can no longer operate as a text in relationship to other past or contemporary texts. It is interesting only to homosexuals. Taken as a symbol or adopted by a political group, the text loses its polysemy, it becomes univocal. This loss of meaning and lack of grip on the textual reality prevents the text from carrying out the only political action that it could: introducing into the textual tissue of the times by way of literature that which it embodies. Doubtless this is why Djuna Barnes dreaded that the lesbians should make her *their* writer, and that by doing this they should reduce her work to one dimension. At all events, and even if Djuna Barnes is read first and widely by lesbians, one should not reduce and limit her to the lesbian minority. This would not only be no favor to her, but also no favor to us. For it is within literature that the work of Barnes can better act both for her and for us.

V

There are texts which are of the greatest strategic importance both in their mode of appearance and their mode of inscription within literary reality. This is true of the whole oeuvre of Barnes, which from this point of view functions as a single, unique text, for *Ryder, Ladies Almanack, Spillway,* and *Nightwood* are linked by correspondences and permutations. Barnes's text is also unique in the sense that it is the first of its kind, and it detonates like a bomb where there has been nothing before it. So it is that, word by word, it has to create its own context, working, laboring with nothing against everything. A text by a minority writer is effective only if it succeeds in making the minority point of view universal, only if it is an important literary text. *Remembrance of Things Past* is a monument of French literature _even though_ homosexuality is *the* theme of the book. Barnes's oeuvre is an important literary oeuvre *even though* her major theme is lesbianism. On the one hand the work of these two writers has transformed, as should all important work, the textual reality of our time. But as the work of members of a minority, their texts have changed the angle of categorization as far as the sociological reality of their group goes, at least in affirming its existence. Before Barnes and Proust how many times had homosexual and lesbian characters been chosen as the theme of literature in general? What had there been in literature between Sappho and Barnes's *Ladies Almanack* and *Nightwood?* Nothing.

V I

The unique context for Djuna Barnes, if one chooses to look at it from a minority angle, was the work of Proust, whom she refers to in *Ladies Almanack*. It is Djuna Barnes who is our Proust (and not Gertrude Stein). A different sort of treatment, nevertheless, was accorded the work of Proust and the work of Barnes: that of Proust more and more triumphant until becoming a classic, that of Barnes appearing like a flash of lightning and then disappearing. Barnes's work is little known, unrecognized in France, but also in the United States. One could say that strategically Barnes is nevertheless more important than Proust. And as such constantly threatened with disappearance. Sappho also has disappeared. But not Plato. One can see quite clearly what is at stake and "dares not speak its name," the name which Djuna Barnes herself abhorred. Sodom is powerful and eternal, said Colette, and Gomorrah doesn't exist. The Gomorrah of *Ladies Almanack,* of *Nightwood,* of "Cassation" and "The Grande Malade" in *Spillway* is a dazzling refutation of Colette's denials, for what is written *is.* "Raise high the roof beam, carpenter, / for here comes the lesbian poet, / rising above the foreign contestants." This poet generally has a hard battle to wage, for, step by step, word by word, she must create her own context in a world which, as soon as she appears, bends every effort to make her disappear. The battle is hard because she must wage it on two fronts: on the formal level with the questions being debated at the moment in literary history, and on the conceptual level against the that-goes-without-saying of the straight mind.

VII

Let us use the word *letter* for what is generally called the signifier and the word *meaning* for what is called the signified (the sign being the combination of the letter and the meaning). Using the words *letter* and *meaning* in place of *signified* and *signifier* permits us to avoid the interference of the referent prematurely in the vocabulary of the sign. (For *signified* and *signifier* describe the sign in terms of the reality being referred to, while *letter* and *meaning* describe the sign solely in relation to language.) In language, only the meaning is abstract. In a work of literary experimentation there can be an equilibrium between letter and meaning. Either there can be an elimination of meaning in favor of the letter ("pure" literary experimentation), or there can be the production of meaning first and foremost. Even in the case of "pure" literary experimentation, it can happen, as Roland Barthes pointed out, that certain meanings are overdetermined to such an extent that the letter is made the meaning and the signifier becomes the signified, whatever the writer does. Minority writers are menaced by the meaning even while they are engaged in formal experimentation: what for them is only a theme in their work, a formal element, imposes itself as meaning *only*, for straight readers. But also it is because the opposition between letter and meaning, between signifier and signified has no *raison d'être* except in an anatomical description of language. In the practice of language, letter and meaning do not act separately. And, for me, a writer's practice consists in constantly reactivating letter and meaning, for, like the letter, meaning vanishes. Endlessly.

VIII

Language for a writer is a special material (compared to that of painters or musicians), since it is used first of all for quite another thing than to produce art and discover forms. It is used by everybody all the time, it is used for speaking and communicating. It is a special material because it is the place, the means, the medium for bringing meaning to light. But meaning hides language from sight. For language, like the purloined letter of Poe's tale, is constantly there, although totally invisible. For one sees, one hears only the meaning. Then isn't meaning language? Yes, it is language, but in its visible and material form, language is form, language is letter. Meaning is not visible, and as such appears to be outside of language. (It is sometimes confused with the referent when one speaks of the "content.") Indeed, meaning is language, but being its abstraction it cannot be seen. Despite this, in the current use of language one sees and hears *only* meaning. It is because the use of language is a very abstract operation, in which at every turn in the production of meaning its form disappears. For when language takes form, it is lost in the literal meaning. It can only reappear abstractly as language while redoubling itself, while forming a figurative meaning, a figure of speech. This, then, is writers' work — to concern themselves with the letter, the concrete, the visibility of language, that is, its material form. Since the time that language has been perceived as material, it has been worked word by word by writers. This work on the level of the words and of the letter reactivates words in their arrangement, and in turn confers on meaning its full meaning: in practice this work brings out in most cases — rather than one meaning — polysemy.

But whatever one chooses to do on the practical level as a writer, when it comes to the conceptual level, there is no other way around — one must assume both a particular *and* a universal point of view, at least to be part of literature. That is, one must work to reach the general, even while starting from an individual or from a specific point of view. This is true for straight writers. But it is true as well for minority writers.

THE TROJAN HORSE

1984

At first it looks strange to the Trojans, the wooden horse, off color, outsized, barbaric. Like a mountain, it reaches up to the sky. Then, little by little, they discover the familiar forms which coincide with those of a horse. Already for them, the Trojans, there have been many forms, various ones, sometimes contradictory, that were put together and worked into creating a horse, for they have an old culture. The horse built by the Greeks is doubtless also one for the Trojans, while they still consider it with uneasiness. It is barbaric for its size but also for its form, too raw for them, the effeminate ones, as Virgil calls them. But later on they become fond of the apparent simplicity, within which they see sophistication. They see, by now, all the elaboration that was hidden at first under a brutal coarseness. They come to see as strong, powerful, the work they had considered formless. They want to make it theirs, to adopt it as a monument and shelter it within their walls, a gratuitous object whose only purpose is to be found in itself. But what if it were a war machine?

Any important literary work is like the Trojan Horse at the time it is produced. Any work with a new form operates as a war machine, because its design and its goal is to pulverize the old forms and formal conventions. It is always produced in hostile territory. And the stranger it appears, nonconforming, unassimilable, the longer it will take for the Trojan Horse to be accepted. Eventually it is adopted, and, even if slowly, it will eventually work like a mine. It will sap and blast out the ground where it was planted. The old literary forms, which everybody was used to, will eventually appear to be outdated, inefficient, incapable of transformation.

When I say that it is quite possible for a work of literature to operate as a war machine upon its epoch, it is not about committed literature that I am talking. Committed literature and *écriture féminine* have in common that they are mythic formations and function like myths, in the sense Barthes gave to this word. As such they throw dust in the eyes of people by amalgamating in the same process two occurrences that do not have the same kind of relationship to the real and to language. I am not speaking thus in the name of ethical reasons. (For example, literature should not be subservient to commitment, for what would happen to the writer if the group which one represents or speaks for stopped being oppressed? Would then the writer have nothing more to say? Or what would happen if the writer's work were banned by the group?) For the question is not an ethical one but a practical one. As one talks about literature, it is necessary to consider all the elements at play. Literary work cannot be influenced directly by history, politics, and ideology because these two fields belong to parallel systems of signs which function differently in the social corpus and use language in a different way. What I see, as soon as language is concerned, is a series of phenomena whose main characteristic is to be totally heterogeneous.

The first irreducible heterogeneity concerns language and its relation to reality. My topic here is the heterogeneity of the social phenomena involving language, such as history, art, ideology, politics. We often try to force them to fit together until they more or less adjust to our conception of what they should be. If I address them separately, I can see that in the expression *committed literature* phenomena whose very nature is different are thrown together. Standing thus, they tend to annul each other. In history, in politics, one is dependent on social history, while in one's work a writer is dependent on literary history, that is, on the history of forms. What is at the center of history and politics is the social body, constituted by the people. What is at the center of literature is forms, constituted by works. Of course people and forms are not at all interchangeable. History is related to people, literature is related to forms.

The first element at hand then for a writer is the huge body of works, past and present—and there are many, very many of them, one keeps forgetting. Modern critics and linguists have by now covered a lot of ground and clarified the subject of literary forms. I think of people like the Russian Formalists, the writers of the *Nouveau Roman*, Barthes, Genette, texts by the *Tel Quel* group. I have a poor knowledge of the state of things in American criticism, but Edgar Allen Poe, Henry James, and Gertrude Stein wrote on the subject. But the fact is that in one's work, one has only two choices—either to reproduce existing forms or to create new ones. There is no other. No writers have been more explicit on this subject than Sarraute for France and Stein for the United States.

The second element at hand for a writer is the raw material, that is, language, in itself a phenomenon heterogeneous both to reality and to its own productions. If one imagines the Trojan Horse as a statue, a form with dimensions, it would be both a material object and a form. But it is exactly what the Trojan Horse is in writing, only in a way a little more intricate, because the material used is language, already a form, but also matter. With writing, words are everything. A good many writers have said it and repeated it, a lot of them are saying it at this very moment, and I say it—words are everything in writing. When one cannot write, it is not, as we often say, that one cannot express one's ideas. It is that one cannot find one's words, a banal situation for writers. Words lie there to be used as raw material by a writer, just as clay is at the disposal of any sculptor. Words are, each one of them, like the Trojan Horse. They are things, material things, and at the same time they mean something. And it is because they mean something that they are abstract. They are a condensate of abstraction and concreteness, and in this they are totally different from all other mediums used to create art. Colors, stone, clay have no meaning, sound has no meaning in music, and very often, most often, no one cares about the meaning they will have when created into a form. One does not expect the meaning to be interesting. One does not expect it to have any meaning at all. While, as soon as something is written down, it must have a meaning. Even in poems a meaning is expected. All the same, a writer needs raw material with which to start one's work, like a painter, a sculptor, or a musician.

This question of language as raw material is not a futile one, since it may help to clarify how in history and in politics the handling of language is different. In history and politics words are taken in their conventional meaning. They are taken only for their meaning, that is in their more abstract form. In literature words are given to be read in their materiality. But one must understand that to attain this result a writer must first reduce language to be as meaningless as possible in order to turn it into a neutral material—that is, a raw material. Only then is one able to work the words into a form. (This does not signify that the finished work has no meaning, but that the meaning comes from the form, the worked words.) A writer must take every word and despoil it of its everyday meaning in order to be able to work with words, on words. Shklovsky, a Russian Formalist, used to say that people stop seeing the different objects that surround them, the trees, the clouds, the houses. They just recognize them without really seeing them. And he said that the task of a writer is to re-create the first powerful vision of things—as opposed to their daily recognition. But he was wrong in that what a writer re-creates is indeed a vision, but the first powerful vision of *words,* not of things. As a writer, I would be totally satisfied if every one of my words had on the reader the same effect, the same shock as if they were being read for the first time. It is what I call dealing a blow with words. As a reader, I find that some writers give me this shock, and it is how I keep on understanding what is happening with words.

What I am saying is that the shock of words in literature does not come out of the ideas they are supposed to promote, since what a writer deals with first is a solid body that must be manipulated in one way or another. And to come back to our horse, if one wants to build a perfect war machine, one must spare oneself the delusion that facts, actions, ideas can dictate directly to words their form. There is a detour, and the shock of words is produced by their association, their disposition, their arrangement, and also by each one of them as used separately. The detour is work, working words as anyone works a material to turn it into something else, a product. There is no way to save this detour in literature, and the detour is what literature is all about.

I said history is related to people, while literature is related to forms. As a discipline, however, history like all disciplines uses language in communicating, writing, reading, understanding, and learning. History, ideology, and politics do not question the medium they use. Their domain is the domain of ideas, which is currently considered to be apart from language, issuing directly from the mind. These disciplines still rest on the classical division of body and soul. Even in the Marxist and post-Marxist traditions, there are, on the one hand, the economic order, the material one, and, on the other hand, ideology and politics, considered as the "superstructure." They do not examine language as a direct exercise of power. In this conception, language, along with art, is part of what they call the superstructure. Both are included in ideology, and as such express nothing but the "ideas" of the ruling class. Without a reexamination of the way language operates both in the domain of ideology and in art, we still remain in what the Marxists precisely call "idealism." Form and content correspond to the body/soul division, and it is applied to the words of language and also to ensembles, that is, to literary works. Linguists speak of signifier and signified, which comes to the same distinction.

Through literature, though, words come back to us whole again. Through literature, then, we can learn something that should be useful in any other field: in words form and content cannot be dissociated, because they partake of the same form, the form of a word, a material form.

One of the best examples of a war machine with a delayed

effect is Proust's work. At first everybody thought it was only a *roman à clef* and a minute description of Parisian high society. The sophisticates feverishly tried to put a name to the characters. Then, in a second stage, they had to change around the women's and men's names, since most of the women in the book were in reality men. They therefore had to take in the fact that a good many of the characters were homosexuals. Since the names were codes for real people, they had to glance back to their apparently normal world, wondering which of them was one, how many of them were, or if they all were. By the end of *Remembrance of Things Past,* it's done. Proust has succeeded in turning the "real" world into a homosexual-only world. It begins with the cohort of the young men populating the embassies, swarming around their leaders like the maids around Queen Esther in Racine. Then come the dukes, the princes, the married men, the servants, the chauffeurs, and all the tradesmen. Everybody ends up being homosexual. There are even a few lesbians, and Colette reproached Proust with having magnified Gomorrah. Saint-Loup, the elegant epitome of a ladies' man, also turns out to be gay. In the last book, Proust, describing the design of the whole work, demonstrates that for him the making of writing is also the making of a particular subject, the constitution of the subject. So that characters and descriptions of given moments are prepared, like so many layers, in order to build, little by little, the subject as being homosexual for the first time in literary history. The song of triumph of *Remembrance* redeems Charlus as well.

For in literature, history, I believe, intervenes at the individual and subjective level and manifests itself in the particular point of view of the writer. It is then one of the most vital and strategic parts of the writer's task to universalize this point of view. But to carry out a literary work one must be modest and know that being gay or anything else is not enough. For reality cannot be directly transferred from the consciousness to the book. The universalization of each point of view demands a particular attention to the formal elements that can be open to history, such as themes, subjects of narratives, as well as the global form of the work. It is the attempted universalization of the point of view that turns or does not turn a literary work into a war machine.

THE MARK OF GENDER

1985

I

The mark of gender, according to grammarians, concerns substantives. They talk about it in terms of function. If they question its meaning, they may joke about it, calling gender a "fictive sex." It is thus that English when compared to French has the reputation of being almost genderless, while French passes for a very gendered language. It is true that, strictly speaking, English does not apply the mark of gender to inanimate objects, to things or nonhuman beings. But as far as the categories of the person are concerned, both languages are bearers of gender to the same extent. Both indeed give way to a primitive ontological concept that enforces in language a division of beings into sexes. The "fictive sex" of nouns or their neuter gender are only accidental developments of this first principle and as such they are relatively harmless.

The manifestation of gender that is identical in English and in French takes place in the dimension of the person. It does not concern only grammarians, although it is a lexical manifestation. As an ontological concept that deals with the nature of Being, along with a whole nebula of other primitive concepts belonging to the same line of thought, gender seems to belong primarily to philosophy. Its *raison d'être* is never questioned in grammar, whose role is to describe forms and functions, not to find a justification for them. It is no longer questioned in philosophy, though, because it belongs to that body of self-evident concepts without which philosophers believe they cannot develop a line of reasoning and which for them go without saying, for they exist prior to any thought, any social order, in nature. So they call gender the lexical delegation of "natural beings," their symbol. Being aware that the notion of gender is not as innocuous as it appears, American feminists use gender as a sociological category, making clear that there is nothing natural about this notion, as sexes have been artificially constructed into political categories — categories of oppression. They have extrapolated the term *gender* from grammar and they tend to superimpose it on the notion of sex. And they are right insofar as gender is the linguistic index of the political opposition between the sexes and of the domination of women. In the same way as sex, man and woman, gender, as a concept, is instrumental in the political discourse of the social contract as heterosexual.

In modern theory, even in the assumptions of disciplines exclusively concerned with language, one remains within the classical division of the concrete world on the one hand, and the abstract one on the other. Physical or social reality and language are disconnected. Abstraction, symbols, signs do not belong to the real. There is on one side the real, the referent, and on the other side language. It is as though the relation to language were a relation of function only and not one of transformation. There is sometimes a confusion between signified and referent, so that they are even used indifferently in certain critical works. Or there is a reduction of the signified to a series of messages, with relays of the referent remaining the only support of the meaning. Among linguists, the Russian Bakhtin, a contemporary of the Russian Formalists whose work has at last been translated, is the only one who seems to me to have a strictly materialist approach to language. In sociolinguistics, there are several developments in this direction, mostly among feminists.[1]

I say that even abstract philosophical categories act upon the real as social. Language casts sheaves of reality upon the social body, stamping it and violently shaping it. For example, the bodies of social actors are fashioned by abstract language as well as by nonabstract language. For there is a plasticity of the real to language: language has a plastic action upon the real. According to Sande Zeig, social gestures are the result of this phenomenon.[2]

About gender, then, it is not only important to dislodge from grammar and linguistics a sociological category that does not speak its name. It is also very important to consider how gender works in language, how gender works upon language, before considering how it works from there upon its users.

Gender takes place in a category of language that is totally unlike any other and which is called the personal pronoun. Personal pronouns are the only linguistic instances that designate the locutors in discourse and their different and successive situations in relationship to that discourse. As such, they are also the pathways and the means of entrance into language. And it is in this sense — that they represent persons — that they interest us here. It is without justification of any kind, without questioning, that personal pronouns somehow engineer gender all through language, taking it along with them quite naturally, so to speak, in any kind of talk, parley, or philosophical treatise. And although they are instrumental in activating the notion of gender, they pass unnoticed. Not being gender-marked themselves in their subjective form (except in one case), they can support the notion of gender while they seem to fulfill another function. In principle, pronouns mark the opposition of gender only in the third person and are not gender bearers, per se, in the other persons. Thus, it is as though gender does not affect them, is not part of their structure, but only a detail in their associated forms. But, in reality, as soon as there is a locutor in discourse, as soon as there is an 'I,' gender manifests itself. There is a kind of suspension of the grammatical form. A direct interpellation of the locutor occurs. The locutor is called upon in person. The locutor intervenes, in the order of the pronouns, without mediation, in *its proper sex* — that is, when the locutor is a sociological woman. One knows that, in French, with *je* ('I'), one must mark the gender as soon as one uses it in relation to past participles and adjectives. In English, where the same kind of obligation does not exist, a locutor, when a sociological woman, must in one way or another, that is, with a certain number of clauses, make her sex public. For gender is the enforcement of sex in language, working in the same way as the declaration of sex in civil status. Gender is not confined within the third person, and the mention of sex in language is not a treatment reserved for the third person. Sex, under the name of gender, permeates the whole body of language and forces every locutor, if she belongs to the oppressed sex, to proclaim it in her speech, that is, to appear in language under her proper physical form and not under the abstract form, which every male locutor has the unquestioned right to use. The abstract form, the general, the universal, this is what the so-called masculine gender means, for the class of men have appropriated the universal for themselves. One must understand that men are not born with a faculty for the universal and that women are not reduced at birth to the particular. The universal has been, and is continually, at every moment, appropriated by men. It does not happen by magic, it must be done. It is an act, a criminal act, perpetrated by one class against another. It is an act carried out at the level of concepts, philosophy, politics. And gender by enforcing upon women a particular category represents a measure of domination. Gender is very harmful to women in the exercise of language. But there is more. Gender is ontologically a total impossibility. For when one becomes a locutor, when one says 'I' and, in so doing, reappropriates language as a whole,[3] proceeding from oneself alone, with the tremendous power to use all language, it is then and there, according to linguists and philosophers, that the supreme act of subjectivity, the advent of subjectivity into consciousness, occurs. It is when starting to speak that one becomes 'I.' This act — the becoming of *the* subject through the exercise of language and through locution — in order to be real, implies that the locutor be an absolute subject. For a relative subject is inconceivable, a relative subject could not speak at all. I mean that in spite of the harsh law of gender and its enforcement upon women, no woman can say 'I' without being for herself a total subject — that is, ungendered, universal, whole. Or, failing this, she is condemned to what I call parrot speech (slaves echoing their masters' talk). Language as a whole gives everyone the same power of becoming an absolute subject through its exercise. But gender, an element of language, works upon this ontological fact to annul it as far as women are concerned and corresponds to a constant attempt to strip them of the most precious thing for a human being — subjectivity. Gender is an ontological impossibility because it tries to accomplish the division of Being. But Being as being is not divided. God or Man as being are One and whole. So what is this divided Being introduced into language through gender? It is an impossible Being, it is a Being that does not exist, an ontological joke, a conceptual maneuver to wrest from women what belongs to them by right: conceiving of oneself as a total subject through the exercise of language. The result of the imposition of gender, acting as a denial at the very moment when one speaks, is to deprive women of the authority of speech, and to force them to make their entrance in a crablike way, particularizing themselves and apologizing profusely. The result is to deny them any claim to the abstract, philosophical, political discourses that give shape to the social body. Gender then must be destroyed. The possibility of its destruction is given through the very exercise of language. For each time I say 'I,' I reorganize the world from my point of view and through abstraction I lay claim to universality. This fact holds true for every locutor.

I I

To destroy the categories of sex in politics and in philosophy, to destroy gender in language (at least to modify its use) is therefore part of my work in writing, as a writer. An important part, since a modification as central as this cannot happen without a transformation of language as a whole. It concerns (touches) words whose meanings and forms are close to, and associated with, gender. But it also concerns (touches) words whose meanings and forms are the furthest away. For once the dimension of the person, around which all others are organized, is brought into play, nothing is left intact. Words, their disposition, their arrangement, their relation to each other, the whole nebula of their constellations shift, are displaced, engulfed or reoriented, put sideways. And when they reappear, the structural change in language makes them look different. They are hit in their meaning and also in their form. Their music sounds different, their coloration is affected. For what is really in question here is a structural change in language, in its nerves, its framing. But language does not allow itself to be worked upon, without parallel work in philosophy and politics, as well as in economics, because, as women are marked in language by gender, they are marked in society as sex. I said that personal pronouns engineer gender through language, and personal pronouns are, if I may say so, the subject matter of each one of my books — except for *Le Brouillon pour un Dictionnaire des Amantes (Lesbian Peoples: Material for a Dictionary)*, written with Sande Zeig. They are the motors for which functioning parts had to be designed, and as such they create the necessity of the form.

The project of *The Opoponax*, my first book, was to work on the subject, the speaking subject, the subject of discourse — subjectivity, generally speaking. I wanted to restore an undivided 'I,' to universalize the point of view of a group condemned to being particular, relegated in language to a subhuman category. I chose childhood as an element of form open to history (it is what a narrative theme is for me), the formation of the ego around language. A massive effort was needed to break the spell of the captured subject. I needed a strong device, something that would immediately be beyond sexes, that the division by sexes would be powerless against, and that could not be coopted. There is in French, as there is in English, a munificent pronoun that is called the indefinite, which means that it is not marked by gender, a pronoun that you are taught in school to systematically avoid. It is *on* in French — *one* in English. Indeed it is so systematically taught that it should not be used that the translator of *The Opoponax* managed never to use it in English. One must say in the translator's favor that it sounds and looks very heavy in English, but no less so in French.

With this pronoun, that is neither gendered nor numbered, I could locate the characters outside of the social division by sexes and annul it for the duration of the book. In French, the masculine form — so the grammarians say — used when a past participle or an adjective is associated with the subject *on,* is in fact neuter. This incidental question of the neuter is in fact very interesting, for even when it is about terms like *l'homme,* like *Man,* grammarians do not speak of neuter in the same sense as they do for *Good* or *Evil,* but they speak of masculine gender. For they have appropriated *l'homme, homo,* whose first meaning is not *male* but *mankind.* For *homo sum.* Man as male is only a derivative and second meaning.[4] To come back to *one, on,* here is a subject pronoun which is very tractable and accommodating since it can be bent in several directions at the same time. First, as already mentioned, it is indefinite as far as gender is concerned. It can represent a certain number of people successively or all at once — everybody, we, they, I, you, people, a small or a large number of persons — and still stay singular. It lends itself to all kinds of substitutions of persons. In the case of *The Opoponax,* it was a delegate of a whole class of people, of everybody, of a few persons, of I (the 'I' of the main character, the 'I' of the narrator, and the 'I' of the reader). *One, on* has been for me the key to the undisturbed use of language, as it is in childhood when words are magic, when words are set bright and colorful in the kaleidoscope of the world, with its many revolutions in the consciousness as one shakes it. *One, on* has been the pathway to the description of the apprenticeship, through words, of everything important to consciousness, apprenticeship in writing being the first, even before the apprenticeship in the use of speech. *One, on,* lends itself to the unique experience of all locutors who, when saying I, can reappropriate the whole language and reorganize the world from their point of view. I did not hide the female characters under male patronyms to make them look more universal, and nevertheless, if I believe what Claude Simon wrote, the attempt at universalization succeeded. He wrote, speaking about what happened to the main character in *The Opoponax,* a little girl: "I see, I breathe, I chew, I feel through her eyes, her mouth, her hands, her skin. . . . I become childhood."[5]

Before speaking of the pronoun which is the axis of *Les Guérillères,* I would like to recall what Marx and Engels said in *The German Ideology* about class interests. They said that each new class that fights for power must, to reach its goal, represent its interest as the common interest of all the members of the society, and that in the philosophical domain this class must give the form of universality to its thought, to present it as the only reasonable one, the only universally valid one.

As for *Les Guérillères,* there is a personal pronoun used very little in French which does not exist in English — the collective plural *elles* (*they* in English) — while *ils* (*they*) often stands for the general: *they say,* meaning *people say.* This general *ils* does

not include *elles,* no more, I suspect, than *they* includes any *she*
in its assumption. One could say that it is a pity that in English
there is not even a hypothetical plural feminine pronoun to try
to make up for the absence of *she* in the general *they*. But what
is the good of it, since when it exists it is not used. The rare
times that it is, *elles* never stands for the general an
bearer of a universal point of view.[6] An *elles* theref
be able to support a universal point of view woul
in literature or elsewhere. In *Les Guérillères,* I try t
the point of view of *elles*. The goal of this appr
feminize the world but to make the categories of s
language. I, therefore, set up *elles* in the text as the
ject of the world. To succeed textually, I needed t
very draconian measures, such as to eliminate, at l
two parts, *he,* or *they-he.* I wanted to produce a shock for the
reader entering a text in which *elles* by its unique presence constitutes an assault, yes, even for female readers. Here again the
adoption of a pronoun as my subject matter dictated the form
of the book. Although the theme of the text was total war, led
by *elles* on *ils,* in order for this new person to take effect, two-
thirds of the text had to be totally inhabited, haunted, by *elles.*
Word by word, *elles* establishes itself as a sovereign subject. Only
then could *il(s), they-he,* appear, reduced and truncated out of
language. This *elles* in order to become real also imposed an epic
form, where it is not only the complete subject of the world but
its conqueror. Another consequence derived from the sovereign
presence of *elles* was that the chronological beginning of the narrative — that is, the total war — found itself in the third part
of the book, and the textual beginning was in fact the end of the
narrative. From there comes the circular form of the book, its

[handwritten margin note: So to destroy sex the feminine POV must be universalized? How does that happen?]

gesta, which the geometrical form of a circle indicates as a modus operandi. In English the translator, lacking the lexical equivalent for *elles,* found himself compelled to make a change, which for me destroys the effect of the attempt. When *elles* is turned into *the women* the process of universalization is destroyed. All of a sudden, *elles* stopped being *mankind.* When one says "the women," one connotes a number of individual women, thus transforming the point of view entirely, by particularizing what I intended as a universal. Not only was my undertaking with the collective pronoun *elles* lost, but another word was introduced, the word *women* appearing obsessively throughout the text, and it is one of those gender-marked words mentioned earlier which I never use in French. For me it is the equivalent of *slave,* and, in fact, I have actively opposed its use whenever possible. To patch it up with the use of a *y* or an *i* (as in *womyn* or *wimmin)* does not alter the political reality of the word. If one tries to imagine *nogger* or *niggir,* instead of *nigger,* one may realize the futility of the attempt. It is not that there is no solution to translating *elles.* There is a solution, although it was difficult for me to find at the time. I am aware that the question is a grammatical one, therefore a textual one, and not a question of translation.[7] The solution for the English translation then is to reappropriate the collective pronoun *they,* which rightfully belongs to the feminine as well as to the masculine gender. *They* is not only a collective pronoun but it also immediately develops a degree of universality which is not immediate with *elles.* Indeed, to obtain it with *elles,* one must produce a work of transformation that involves a whole pageant of other words and that touches the imagination. *They* does not partake of the naturalistic, hysterical

[handwritten marginal note: language must be changed • we will fight to find the right terms]

bent that accompanies the feminine gender. *They* helps to go beyond the categories of sex. But *they* can be effective in my design only when it stands by itself, like its French counterpart. Only with the use of *they* will the text regain its strength and strangeness. The fact that the book begins with the end and that the end is the chronological beginning will be textually justified by the unexpected identity of *they*. In the third part, the war section, *they* cannot be shared by the category to be eliminated from the general. In a new version the masculine gender must be more systematically particularized than it is in the actual form of the book. The masculine must not appear under *they* but only under *man, he, his,* in analogy with what has been done for so long to the feminine gender *(woman, she, her)*. It seems to me that the English solution will take us even a step further in making the categories of sex obsolete in language.

Talking about the key pronoun of *The Lesbian Body (Le Corps lesbien)* is a very difficult task for me, and sometimes I have considered this text a reverie about the beautiful analysis of the pronouns *je* and *tu* by the linguist Emile Benveniste. The bar in the *j/e* of *The Lesbian Body* is a sign of excess. A sign that helps to imagine an excess of 'I,' an 'I' exalted. 'I' has become so powerful in *The Lesbian Body* that it can attack the order of heterosexuality in texts and assault the so-called love, the heroes of love, and lesbianize them, lesbianize the symbols, lesbianize the gods and the goddesses, lesbianize the men and the women. This 'I' can be destroyed in the attempt and resuscitated. Nothing resists this 'I' (or this *tu*, which is its same, its love), which spreads itself in the whole world of the book, like a lava flow that nothing can stop.

To understand my undertaking in this text, one must go back to *The Opoponax*, in which the only appearance of the narrator comes with a *je*, 'I,' located at the end of the book in a small sentence untranslated[8] in English, a verse of Maurice Scève, in *La Délie*: *"Tant je l'aimais qu'en elle encore je vis"* (I loved her so that in her I live still). This sentence is the key to the text and pours its ultimate light upon the whole of it, demystifying the meaning of the opoponax and establishing a lesbian subject as the absolute subject while lesbian love is the absolute love. *On,* the opoponax, and the *je*, 'I' of the end have narrow links. They function by relays. First *on* completely coincides with the character Catherine Legrand as well as with the others. Then the opoponax appears as a talisman, a sesame to the opening of the world, as a word that compels both words and world to make sense, as a metaphor for the lesbian subject. After the repeated assertions of Catherine Legrand that I *am the opoponax* the narrator can at the end of the book take the relay and affirm in her name: "I loved her so that in her I live still." The chain of permutations from the *on* to the *je*, 'I,' of *The Opoponax* has created a context for the 'I' in *The Lesbian Body*. This understanding both global and particular, both universal and unique, brought from within a perspective given in homosexuality, is the object of some extraordinary pages by Proust.

To close my discussion of the notion of gender in language, I will say that it is a mark unique of its kind, the unique lexical symbol that refers to an oppressed group. No other has left its trace within language to such a degree that to eradicate it would not only modify language at the lexical level but would upset the structure itself and its functioning. Furthermore, it would change the relations of words at the metaphorical level far beyond the very few concepts and notions that are touched upon by this transformation. It would change the coloration of words in relation to each other and their tonality. It is a transformation that would affect the conceptual-philosophical level and the political one as well as the poetic one.

THE SITE OF ACTION

1984

What has been taking place in Nathalie Sarraute's work since *Les Fruits d'or* (*The Golden Fruit,* 1963) is so total a transformation of the substance of the novel that it is difficult to grasp it as such. As it has the volatility of spoken words, I will call the material with which she works — in order to establish a comparison with what linguists call "locution" — "interlocution." By this word, infrequently used in linguistics, I imply all that occurs between people when they speak. It includes the phenomenon, in its entirety, which goes beyond speech proper. And as the meaning of this word derives from *interrupt,* to *cut someone short,* that which does not designate a mere speech act, I extend it to any action linked to the use of speech: to accidents of discourse (pauses, excess, lack, tone, intonation) and to effects relating to it (tropisms, gestures).

In this perspective, Sarraute's characters are interlocutors: More anonymous even than Kafka's K., they have the tenor of Plato's Georgias, Crito, Euthyphro. Called forth by dialogue and the same philosophical necessity, they disappear like meteorites or like people we pass in the street, people who are neither more nor less real than characters of a novel and who are bedecked with a name to satisfy the needs of our inner fiction. But what matters here over and above those interlocutors who, for the reader, are ordinary characters, ordinary propositions, is Sarraute's philosophical matter, the locution and the interlocution, what she herself, with regard to the novel, calls "l'usage de la parole" [the use of speech]. Unlike linguistics, which has but one anatomical point of view on language, the point of view of the novel does not have to impose limits on itself for it can collect, gather, in a single movement, causes, effects, and actors. With Sarraute, the novel creates phenomena in literature which as yet have no name, either in science or philosophy.

It must first be noted that all those problems relating to character, to point of view, to dialogue, which Sarraute developed in *L'Ere du soupçon* (*The Age of Suspicion*, 1956), have been resolved by the fact that the use of speech has become the exclusive theme of her books. The character, totally changed in its form, was still too cumbersome for the needs of the text. This form itself has disappeared. The spatiotemporal universe, which generally constitutes a pregnant element in fiction (description of places, of buildings, of precise geographical spaces) and which was already very restricted in the novels of Sarraute preceding *Les Fruits d'or*, is now the most abstract that it can be: it is any unspecified place where one speaks, or else, perhaps, a mental space with imaginary interlocutors.

Sometimes an interlocutor breaks off, drops the conversation, and withdraws to undetermined places. Sometimes, too, there is a "here" and a "there," but this indication of distance does not correspond to place, but to a disparity at work in the language: Those people there and these people here are not speaking the same language. The point of view, far from being unique, is constantly and quickly shifting, according to the interlocutors' interventions, provoking changes of meaning, variations. The multiplicity of this point of view and its mobility are produced and sustained by the rhythm of the writing that is broken up by what is called discourse and its accidents. It is important to emphasize this multiplicity as far as the psychological, ethical, or political interpretation of the characters is concerned, for no interpretation is possible. It is, on the contrary, continually prevented. Not one of the spoken discourses, not even the inner dialogues or the inner discourses, is assumed by the author and, further, there is no privileged interlocutor entrusted with her point of view (contrary to Plato's Socrates), that which forces the reader to adopt them all successively, as temporary scenarios, as in *Martereau,* for example. Thus "le lecteur, sans cesse tendu, aux aguets, comme s'il était à la place de celui à qui les paroles s'adressent, mobilise tous ses instincts de défense, tous ses dons d'intuition, sa mémoire, ses facultés de jugement et de raisonnement" [the reader, who has remained intent, on the lookout, as though he were in the shoes of the person to whom the words are directed, mobilizes all his instincts of defense, all his powers of intuition, his memory, his faculties of judgment and reasoning].[1]

I would delight in speaking of the very substance of the text itself, of the rhythm, the sequences, and their mode of development, of the use of words as isolated words dispersing between interlocutors, of the spectacular oscillations of the text at moments when shifts in point of view take place, of the interlocutory sequences, of the clichés that are orchestrated around a word, as though by baton, of the birth and deployment in counterpoint of a text. This text responds like some kind of antique Greek choir, not tragic but sarcastic, commenting on the fortuities of the discourse, of the dynamic gathering of all the elements in a unique movement that carries them all away and which is the text.

But I must speak of a more philosophical matter. That is why I mentioned Plato, although, contrary to his interlocutors, Sarraute's do not deliver it as a whole.

The use of speech, such as it is practiced everyday, is an operation that suffocates language and thus the ego, whose deadly stake is the hiding, the dissimulating, as carefully as possible, of the nature of language. What is caught unaware here and suffocates are the words between the words, before the "fathers," before the "mothers," before the "you's," before "the arising of the dead," before "structuralisma," before "capitalisma." What is smothered by all kinds of talk, whether it be that of the street or of the philosopher's study, is the first language (of which the dictionary gives us an approximate idea): the one in which meaning has not yet occurred, the one which is for all, which belongs to all, and which everyone in turn can take, use, bend toward a meaning. For this is the social pact that binds us, the exclusive contract (none other is possible), a social contract that exists just as Rousseau imagined it, one where the "right of the strongest" is a contradiction in terms, one where there are neither men nor women, neither races nor oppression, nothing but what can be named progressively, word by word, language. Here we are all free and equal or there would be no possible pact. We all learned to speak with the awareness that words can be exchanged, that language forms itself in a relation of absolute reciprocity. If not, who would be mad enough to want to talk? The tremendous power — such as linguists have made it known to us — the power to use, proceeding from oneself alone, all language, with its words of dazzling sounds and meanings, belongs to us all. Language exists as the commonplace[2] where one can revel freely and, in one stroke, through words, offer to others at arm's length the same license, one without which there would be no meaning. "Par toutes leurs voyelles, par toutes leurs consonnes [les mots] se tendent, s'ouvrent, aspirent, s'imbibent, s'emplissent, se gonflent, s'épandent à la mesure d'espaces infinis, à la mesure de bonheurs sans bornes" [With all their vowels, their consonants, (words) stretch, open up, inhale, become saturated, fill up, swell, spread over infinite space, over boundless happinesses.[3]

Language exists as a paradise made of visible, audible, palpable, palatable words:

quand le fracas des mots heurtés les uns contre les autres couvre leur sens . . . quand frottés les uns contre les autres, ils le recouvrent de gerbes étincelantes . . . quand dans chaque mot son sens réduit à un petit noyau est entouré de vastes étendues brumeuses . . . quand il est dissimulé par un jeu de reflets, de réverbérations, de miroitements . . . quand les mots entourés d'un halo semblent voguer suspendus à distance les uns des autres . . . quand se posant en nous un par un, ils s'implantent, s'imbibent lentement de notre plus obscure substance, nous emplissent tout entiers, se dilatent, s'épandent à notre mesure, au-delà de notre mesure, hors de toute mesure?

[when the clash of words colliding with one another drowns their meaning . . . when, rubbed together, they produce a shower of sparks which conceals it . . . when the meaning of each word is reduced to a tiny kernel surrounded by vast, misty spaces . . . when it is hidden under the play of reflections, of reverberations, of scintillations . . . when words are surrounded by a halo and seem to float, suspended at a distance from one another . . . when they settle into us one by one, embed themselves, slowly imbibe our most obscure substance, fill our every nook and cranny, dilate, spread to our measure, beyond our measure, beyond all measure?][4]

But even while the social contract, such as it is, guarantees the entire and exclusive disposition of language to everyone, and while, in accordance with this same right, it guarantees the possibility of its exchange with any interlocutor on the same terms — for the very fact that the exchange is possible guarantees reciprocity — it nevertheless appears that the two modes of relating to language have nothing in common. It is almost as though, suddenly, instead of there being one contract, there were two. In one, the explicit contract — the one where the "I" is made a human being by being given the use of speech, the one where the practice of language is constitutive of the "I" who speaks it — face to face with words, "I" is a hero *(héros — héraut, Hérault, erre haut)*[5] to which the world, which it forms and deforms at will, belongs. And everyone agrees to grant this right to the "I"; it is a universal agreement. Here, I do not have to stand on ceremony, I can put my boots on the table, I am almighty, or as Pinget says in *Baga,* I am the "roi de moi" [I am my own king]. In the other contract, the implicit one, the very opposite takes place. With the appearance of an interlocutor, the poles are reversed:

Disons que ce qui pourrait les faire céder à ce besoin de fuite . . . nous l'avons tous éprouvé . . . ce serait la perspective de ce à quoi elles seront obligées de se soumettre . . . cette petite opération . . . Petite? Mais à quoi bon essayer raisonnablement, docilement, décemment, craintivement, de s'abriter derrière "petite"? Soyons francs, pas petite, pas petite du tout . . . le mot qui lui convient est "énorme" . . . une énorme opération, une véritable mue.

[Let us say that what might make them give way to this need to escape . . . we have all felt it . . . would be the prospect of what they would be obliged to submit to . . . that little operation . . . Little? But what good is it to try — reasonably, docilely, decently, fearfully — to

take refuge behind "little"? Let us be frank, not little, not little as all
... the appropriate word is "enormous" ... an enormous operation,
a veritable molt.][6]

That the other advances in his own words is sufficient for the
"I," even before it utters a word, to be thrown a robe which is
anything but a royal cloak:

D'elle quelque chose se dégage ... comme un fluide ... comme des
rayons ... il sent que sous leur effet il subit une opération par laquelle il est mis en forme, qui lui donne un corps, un sexe, un âge,
l'affuble d'un signe comme une formule mathématique résumant un
long développement.

[Something emanates from her ... Something like a fluid, like rays
... under whose effect he feels he is undergoing an operation which
gives him a form, which gives him a body, a sex, an age, rigs him out
with a sign like a mathematical formula that sums up a long development.][7]

Even before "I" knows it, "I" is made a prisoner, it becomes the
victim of a fool's deal. What it has mistaken for absolute liberty,
the necessary reciprocity, without which language is impossible,
is but the surrender, a deal that overthrows the "I" at the mercy
of the slightest word. That this word be uttered and

le centre, le lieu secret où se trouvait l'état-major et d'où lui, chef su-
prême, les cartes étalées sous les yeux, examinant la configuration du
terrain, écoutant les rapports, prenant les décisions, dirigeait les opér-
ations, une bombe l'a soufflé ... il est projeté à terre, ses insignes ar-
rachés, il s'est secoué, contraint à se relever et à marcher, poussé à
coups de crosse, à coups de pied dans le troupeau grisâtre des captifs,
tous portant la même tenue, classés dans la même catégorie.

[The center, the secret spot where the General Staff is located and
from where he, the Commander-in-Chief, all the maps spread out for
him to see, examining the lay of the land, listening to reports, taking

decisions, directing operations, a bomb hit it . . . he is thrown to the ground, his insignia torn off, he is shaken, obliged to get up and walk, pushed forward, by blows from rifle butts, kicks, into the gray flock of the prisoners, all dressed alike, classified in the same category.][8]

In the second contract, the implicit one, in the interlocution no holds are barred and may the strongest win, he deserves it. To speak of one's right would be inappropriate in this case, for one is the strongest only by taking advantage of the unlimited power over the other granted by language, a power all the more unlimited because it has no recognized social existence. It is, therefore, with complete impunity that the strongest in words can become a criminal. Words, *les paroles,*

pourvu qu'elles présentent une apparence à peu près anodine et banale peuvent être et sont souvent en effet, sans que personne y trouve à redire, sans que la victime ose clairement se l'avouer, l'arme quotidienne, insidieuse et très efficace, d'innombrables petits crimes. Car rien n'égale la vitesse avec laquelle elles touchent l'interlocuteur au moment où il est le moins sur ses gardes, ne lui donnant souvent qu'une sensation de chatouillement désagréable ou de légère brûlure, la précision avec laquelle elles vont droit en lui aux points les plus secrets et les plus vulnérables, se logent dans ses replis les plus profonds, sans qu'il ait le désir, ni les moyens, ni le temps de riposter.

[provided they present a more or less harmless, commonplace appearance, can be and, in fact, without anyone's taking exception, without the victim's even daring to admit it frankly himself . . . often are the daily, insidious, and very effective weapon responsible for countless minor crimes. For there is nothing to equal the rapidity with which they attain to the other person at the moment when he is least on his guard, often giving him merely the sensation of disagreeable tickling or slight burning; or the precision with which they enter straight into him at his most secret and vulnerable points, and lodge in his innermost recesses, without his having the desire, the means, or the time to retort.][9]

With the turn of a word, one is brought into line and led between two gentlemen, like the narrator in *Martereau,* for that which, in accord with the primary pact, establishes the "I" as free, now holds it bound hand and foot. Winged words are also bludgeons, language is a lure, paradise is also the hell of discourses, no longer the confusion of languages as in Babel, or discord, but the grand ordinance, the bringing into line of a strict meaning, of a social meaning.

What is taking place between the two contracts? Why is it that, at any moment, no longer almighty subject, no longer king, "I" can find itself rolling in the dust at the foot of the throne? When Sartre spoke in the preface to *Portrait d'un inconnu (Portrait of a Man Unknown,* 1956) of the "va et vient incessant du particulier au général" [incessant coming and going from the particular to the general], that which is the approach of any science, he was thinking of the tropisms, of this movement of consciousness, of this indicator of a reaction to one or several words, and he was imagining a particular consciousness trying to reach the general. Actually, however, it is just the contrary, since each time "I" is spoken in the singular, it is then, according to Sarraute, that "I" is the general, an "infinite," a "nebula," a "world." And one interlocutor, only one, is sufficient for the "I" to pass from the general to a simple particular in a movement that is exactly the reverse of that attributed to science.

It is there, in the interval between locution and interlocution, that the conflict emerges: the strange wrenching, the tension in the movement from particular to general, experienced by any human being when from an "I" — unique in language, shapeless, boundless, infinite — it suddenly becomes nothing or almost nothing, "you," "he," "she," "a small, rather ugly fellow," an interlocutor. The brutal reduction (a "véritable mue" [true molt]) implies that the so-promising contract was glaringly false. And thus, for Sarraute, it implies not only that the social meaning or the contradictions between the general interest and the particular interest, in exercising a constant pressure over the exchange of language, particularly in the interlocution, are at the origin of the conflict; it is also toward the entire system that Sarraute turns the interrogation: toward the *fundamental flaw* in the contract, the worm in the fruit, toward the fact that the contract in its very structure is an impossibility — given that, through language, "I" is at once everything, "I" has every power (as a locutor), and that, suddenly, there is the downfall wherein "I" loses all power (as an interlocutor) and is endangered by words that can cause madness, kill. The social significance, the commonplaces are not the cause: they come after, and are used. It even seems that that is what they are there for, "one has only to draw from the common stock." Moreover, they are at everyone's disposal, everyone makes fervent use of them, the weak, the strong, each, in his own way, playing the victim, the cocky one, the model young couple, the self-assured man, without there being any winners or losers. The reductive "you" which levels them, demeans them, labels them "honteuses et rougissantes dans leur ridicule nudité, esclaves anonymes enchaînées l'une à l'autre, bétail conduit pêle-mêle au marché" [ashamed and blushing in their ridiculous nudity, anonymous slaves chained one to the other, cattle led pell-mell to the market][10] can, like a boomerang, turn back on the aggressor, as is the case in *Martereau,* where the powerful one, in turn, becomes impoverished: "tendre faible transi de froid . . . les gamins lui jettent des pierres. . . . La face peinte, affublé d'oripeaux grotesques, elle le force chaque soir à faire le pitre, à crier cocórico sur l'estrade d'un beuglant, sous les rires, les huées." [Tender, weak, numb with cold . . . the street urchins throw stones at him. . . . With his face painted, rigged out in an absurd get-up, she forces him each evening to play the clown, to crow "cock-a-doodle-do" on the stage of a cheap cabaret, while the audience howls and hoots.][11]

Any social actor makes use of this weapon of commonplaces, whatever his situation, for it is the debased form of reciprocity that has founded the exchange contract. But the conflict due to the confrontation of the two modes of relation to language (locution and interlocution) remains, nevertheless, insurmountable, from whatever point of view.

The substance of Sarraute's novels envelops this double movement, this <u>deadly</u> embrace, with its violent, vehement, passionate words. That is what leads me to say that the paradise of the social contract exists only in literature, where the tropisms, by their violence, are able to counter any reduction of the "I" to a common denominator, to tear open the closely woven material of the commonplaces, and to continually prevent their organization into a system of compulsory meaning.

soc contract exists
only through creativity
+ imagination in
lit. • she can
counter the labels+
hold on to her "I"

Foreword

1. Cf. Charlotte Bunch, "Learning from Lesbian Separatism," *Ms.* (November 1976).
2. Ariane Brunet and Louise Turcotte, "Separatism and Radicalism: An Analysis of the Differences and Similarities," trans. Lee Heppner, in *For Lesbians Only: A Separatist Anthology* (London: Onlywomen Press, 1988), p. 450.
3. Adrienne Rich, "Compulsory Heterosexuality and Lesbian Existence," *Signs* 5, no. 4 (Summer 1980).
4. Rich, p. 648.
5. Rich, p. 659.

The Category of Sex

1. André Breton, *Le Premier Manifeste du Surréalisme,* 1924.
2. Pleasure in sex is no more the subject of this paper than is happiness in slavery.

One Is Not Born a Woman

1. Christine Delphy, "Pour un féminisme matérialiste," *L'Arc* 61 (1975). Translated as "For a Materialist Feminism," *Feminist Issues* 1, no. 2 (Winter 1981).

2. Colette Guillaumin, "Race et Nature: Système des marques, idée de groupe naturel et rapports sociaux," *Pluriel*, no. 11 (1977). Translated as "Race and Nature: The System of Marks, the Idea of a Natural Group and Social Relationships," *Feminist Issues* 8, no. 2 (Fall 1988).

3. I use the word society with an extended anthropological meaning; strictly speaking, it does not refer to societies, in that lesbian societies do not exist completely autonomously from heterosexual social systems.

4. Simone de Beauvoir, *The Second Sex* (New York: Bantam, 1952), p. 249.

5. Redstockings, *Feminist Revolution* (New York: Random House, 1978), p. 18.

6. Andrea Dworkin, "Biological Superiority: The World's Most Dangerous and Deadly Idea," *Heresies* 6:46.

7. Ti-Grace Atkinson, *Amazon Odyssey* (New York: Links Books, 1974), p. 15.

8. Dworkin, op. cit.

9. Guillaumin, op. cit.

10. de Beauvoir, op. cit.

11. Guillaumin, op. cit.

12. Dworkin, op. cit.

13. Atkinson, p. 6: "If feminism has any logic at all, it must be working for a sexless society."

14. Rosalind Rosenberg, "In Search of Woman's Nature," *Feminist Studies* 3, no. 1/2 (1975): 144.

15. Ibid., p. 146.

16. In an article published in *L'Idiot International* (mai 1970), whose original title was "Pour un mouvement de libération des femmes" ("For a Women's Liberation Movement").

17. Christiane Rochefort, *Les stances à Sophie* (Paris: Grasset, 1963).

The Straight Mind

1. This text was first read in New York at the Modern Language Association Convention in 1978 and dedicated to American lesbians.

2. However, the classical Greeks knew that there was no political power without mastery of the art of rhetoric, especially in a democracy.

3. Throughout this paper, when Lacan's use of the term "the Unconscious" is referred to it is capitalized, following his style.

4. For example see Karla Jay and Allen Young, eds., *Out of the Closets* (New York: Links Books, 1972).

5. Heterosexuality: a word which first appears in the French language in 1911.

6. Ti-Grace Atkinson, *Amazon Odyssey* (New York: Links Books, 1974), pp. 13–23.

7. Claude Faugeron and Philippe Robert, *La Justice et son public et les représentations sociales du système pénal* (Paris: Masson, 1978).

8. See, for her definition of "social sex," Nicole-Claude Mathieu, "Notes pour une définition sociologique des catégories de sexe," *Epistémologie Sociologique* 11 (1971). Translated as *Ignored by Some, Denied by Others: The Social Sex Category in Sociology* (pamphlet), Explorations in Feminism 2 (London: Women's Research and Resources Centre Publications, 1977), pp. 16–37.

9. In the same way that in every other class struggle the categories of opposition are "reconciled" by the struggle whose goal is to make them disappear.

10. Are the millions of dollars a year made by the psychoanalysts symbolic?

11. Roland Barthes, *Mythologies* (New York: Hill and Wang, 1972), p. 11.

On the Social Contract

1. *The Social Contract, or Principles of Political Right* (1762), by J.-J. Rousseau, citizen of Geneva.

2. Colette Guillaumin, "Pratique du pouvoir et idée de Nature: 1. L'appropriation des femmes; 2. Le discours de la Nature," *Questions*

féministes n°2 et n°3 (1978). Translated as "The Practice of Power and Belief in Nature: 1. The Appropriation of Women; 2. The Naturalist Discourse," *Feminist Issues* 1, nos. 2 and 3 (Winter and Summer 1981).

3. See Colette Capitan Peter, "A Historical Precedent for Patriarchal Oppression: 'The Old Regime' and the French Revolution," *Feminist Issues* 4, no. 1 (Spring 1984): 83–89.

4. See "The Straight Mind" and "One Is Not Born a Woman," this volume.

5. This statement by Marx and Engels is particularly relevant to the modern situation.

6. See Aristotle, *The Politics.*

7. Nicole-Claude Mathieu, "Quand céder n'est pas consentir. Des déterminants matériels et psychiques de la conscience dominée des femmes, et de quelques-unes de leurs interprétations en ethnologie," in *L'Arraisonnement des femmes, Essais en anthropologie des sexes* (Paris: Editions de l'Ecole des Hautes Etudes en Sciences Sociales, 1985). Translated as "When Yielding Is Not Consenting. Material and Psychic Determinants of Women's Dominated Consciousness and Some of Their Interpretation in Ethnology," *Feminist Issues* 9, no. 2 (1989), part I.

8. Jean Paulhan, "Happiness in Slavery," preface to *The Story of O,* by Pauline de Réage.

Homo Sum

1. We must add here the notion of the "fourth world" used in Europe to designate people who live in poverty in the Western industrialized world.

2. Nasty tricks, circumventing tricks.

The Point of View

1. The beginning of the women's liberation movement in France and everywhere else was in itself a questioning of the categories of sex. But afterwards only radical feminists and lesbians continued to challenge on political and theoretical grounds the use of the sexes as categories

and as classes. For the theoretical aspect of this question, see *Questions féministes* between 1977 and 1980 and *Feminist Issues* since its first number.

2. See Colette Guillaumin, "The Masculine: Denotations/Connotations," *Feminist Issues* 5, no. 1 (Spring 1985).

3. Nathalie Sarraute, *The Age of Suspicion* (New York: George Braziller, 1963), p. 57.

4. Ibid.

5. Sappho, Book IX, pp. 110–111.

The Trojan Horse

1. Gertrude Stein, *How to Write* (New York: Dover, 1975).

The Mark of Gender

1. Colette Guillaumin, "The Question of Difference," *Feminist Issues* 2, no. 1 (1982); "The Masculine: Denotations/Connotations," *Feminist Issues* 5, no. 1 (Spring 1985); Nicole-Claude Mathieu, "Masculinity/Feminity," *Feminist Issues* 1, no. 1 (Summer 1980); "Biological Paternity, Social Maternity," *Feminist Issues* 4, no. 1 (Spring 1984).

2. Sande Zeig, "The Actor as Activator," 5, *Feminist Issues* 5, no. 1 (Spring 1985).

3. Cf. Emile Benveniste, *Problems in General Linguistics* (Coral Gables, FL: University of Miami Press, 1971).

4. The first demonstration of the women's liberation movement in France took place at the Arc de Triomphe, where the grave of the unknown soldier is located. Among the mottos on the banners, one read: *Un homme sur deux est une femme* (one man in two is a woman). The purpose of the demonstration was to lay a wreath in honor of the wife of the unknown soldier (more unknown even than the soldier), and it took place in support of the American women's demonstration of August 1970.

5. In *L'Express*, 30 novembre 1964.

6. Nathalie Sarraute uses *elles* very often throughout her work. But it is not to make it stand for a universal, her work being of another nature. I am convinced that, without her use, *elles* would not have imposed itself upon me with such force. It is an example of what Julia Kristeva calls intertextuality.

7. Indeed David Le Vay's translation is a beautiful one, particularly for the rhythm of the sentences and the choice of the vocabulary.

8. *The Opoponax* in English is deprived of the complete body of poetry which in French was incorporated into the text as an organic element. It was not differentiated by italics or quotation marks. In English this complete body of poetry stands out untranslated and has no operative virtue whatsoever.

The Site of Action

1. Nathalie Sarraute, *L'Ere du soupçon* (Paris: Gallimard, 1956), p. 144; English trans., *The Age of Suspicion,* trans. Maria Jolas (New York: George Braziller, 1963), p. 115.

2. [Translator's note: By "lieu commun" Wittig evokes her both the common place, as in a communal place, and the *commonplace,* as in a platitude of language. This desired ambiguity is lost in written English (though not in spoken English), where a choice must be made between the two.]

3. Nathalie Sarraute, *Disent les imbéciles* (Paris: Gallimard, 1976), p. 130. English trans., *Fools Say,* trans. Maria Jolas (New York: George Braziller, 1977), pp. 101–102.

4. Nathalie Sarraute, *L'Usage de la parole* (Paris: Gallimard, 1980), p. 148. English trans., *The Use of Speech,* trans. Barbara Wright, in consultation with the author (New York: George Braziller, 1983), p. 142.

5. [Translator's note: The homonymic pun on "héros" (hero) is not translatable.]

6. Sarraute, *L'Usage de la parole,* pp. 88–89 (English trans., *The Use of Speech,* p. 85).

7. Ibid., p. 91. (English trans., p. 87).

8. Sarraute, *Disent les Imbéciles,* p. 42 (English trans., *Fools Say,* p. 35).

9. Sarraute, *L'Ere du soupçon,* pp. 122–123 (English trans., *The Age of Suspicion,* pp. 97–98).

10. Nathalie Sarraute, *Martereau* (Paris: Gallimard, 1953; Le livre de poche, 1964), p. 129. English trans., *Martereau,* trans. Maria Jolas (New York: George Braziller, 1959), p. 127.

11. Ibid., p. 213 (English trans., pp. 211–212).

Bibliography

Other works by Monique Wittig

Books

The Opoponax. New York: Simon and Schuster, 1966; Daughters,
1976. Originally published as *L'Opoponax* (Paris: Editions de
Minuit, 1964; Le livre de poche, 1971). Winner of the Prix de
Medicis, 1964. The book has been published in twelve countries.

Les Guérillères. New York: Viking, 1971; Avon, 1973; Boston: Beacon Press, 1986. Originally published in France (Paris: Editions de
Minuit, 1969). The book has been published in eight countries.

The Lesbian Body. New York: William Morrow, 1975; Avon, 1976;
Boston: Beacon Press, 1986. Originally published as *Le Corps lesbien* (Paris: Editions de Minuit, 1973). The book has been published in seven countries.

Lesbian Peoples: Material for a Dictionary, co-authored with Sande
Zeig. Translated by the authors. New York: Avon, 1979. Originally
published as *Brouillon pour un dictionnaire des Amantes* (Paris:
Grasset, 1975). The book has been published in six countries.

Across the Acheron. London: Peter Owen, 1987. Originally published
as *Virgile, non* (Paris: Editions de Minuit, 1985). Also published in
the Netherlands.

Short stories

"Banlieues." *Nouveau Commerce* (1965).
"Voyage." *Nouvelle Revue Francaise* (1967).

"Une partie de campagne." *Nouveau Commerce* (1970).

Untitled. *Minuit* (1972).

"Un jour mon prince viendra." *Questions féministes* (1978).

"Tchiches et Tchouches." In *Le Genre Humain* (Paris: Centre national de la recherche sociologique, 1983). Written for a conference at La Maison francaise of New York University, March 1982.

"Paris-la-Politique." *Vlasta* (1985).

Plays

L'Amant Vert. 1967. Produced in Bolivia, 1969.

Le Grand Cric-Jules, Récreation, Dialogue pour les deux frères et la soeur. Short plays commissioned by Stuttgart Radio.

The Constant Journey. First produced in the United States in 1984, and in France as *Le Voyage sans fin* at the Theatre du Rond-Point, 1985. Co-director with Sande Zeig. A video of this play was made by the Centre audio-visuel Simone de Beauvoir and is now in the collection of film and tape at the Lincoln Center Library for the Performing Arts.

Theory and criticism

"Lacunary Films." *New Statesman* (1966). On Godard.

"Bouvard et Pécuchet." *Les Cahiers Madeleine Renaud-Barrault* (1967). On Flaubert.

"Paradigm." In *Homosexualities and French Literature.* Ithaca: Cornell University Press, 1979.